THE SECRET
MILLIONAIRE

THE SECRET MILLIONAIRE

I kept my £10 million lottery win a secret until I knew my sweetheart loved me … This is my story

Joe Johnson

With John McShane

JOHN BLAKE

ISBN: 978 1 84454 557 5

British Library Cataloguing-in-Publication Data:

A catalogue record for this book is available from the British Library.

Design by www.envydesign.co.uk

Printed in the by CPI Bookmarque, Croydon, CR0 4TD

1 3 5 7 9 10 8 6 4 2

Papers used by John Blake Publishing are natural, recyclable products
made from wood grown in sustainable forests. The manufacturing processes
conform to the environmental regulations of the country of origin.

Every attempt has been made to contact the relevant copyright-holders,
but some were unobtainable. We would be grateful if the appropriate
people could contact us.

To the love of my life, my wife Lisa, and to my wonderful children: Nick, Tina, Zak, Alfie and Blue.

I would also like to dedicate this book to my inspiration and dear friend Aroon Maharajh. I only knew him a short while, but felt like I'd known him a lifetime and wish I had. A sad loss too soon…until we meet again.

A poem to Lisa:

The life that I have
Is all that I have
And the life that I have
Is yours.

The love that I have
Of the life that I have
Is yours and yours and yours.

('The Life That I Have' by Leo Marks)

Contents

Acknowledgements

The greatest thanks to my dear brother Danny and wife Stella, who were there for me and the children in my early days. Also to my brother Charlie and wife Maisie. A special thanks to my dear mother-in-law Shirley, who sadly passed away recently, who was like my own mother and whom I miss very much. To Lisa's partner-in-crime, the great organiser, her sister Josie. To Lisa's sister Lorraine, who has always been there for me. And deep gratitude to Lysa for helping to bring us together.

To my dear friends Francine and Elizabeth Cardona (Alicia), who always lent an ear in time of troubles and who appreciate loyalty and friendship. To friends in Spain: Jan and Terry, Michelle and John, Leeza and Rob, Solly and Margaret, Ross and Sandy, and gypsy Kathy. If we didn't have such lovely friends here in Spain we would probably be back in the UK – so a huge 'thank you'.

Also to my agent and friend Aroon, a big 'thanks' – I couldn't have done it without you, mate. And finally to John McShane, my co-author, thank you for all your help and patience during the writing of my story.

Prologue

The woman I loved was busy in the kitchen.

As I watched Lisa wearily peeling the potatoes and preparing the green vegetables for the pans that were already brim-filled with water, I wondered if now was the right moment to tell her my secret.

She brushed the long, Scandinavian-blonde hair from her face as she reached a tired but elegant arm up to find the bottle of mint sauce that would give the small joint of lamb that little extra dash of flavour. Then she placed the joint in the already-warm oven and made sure the table was properly laid with the plates, knives and forks in their right place before she rested for a moment. I could hardly take my eyes off her as I poured her a glass of red wine.

It had been a hard day for her, working as she did in a busy high street café from early morning until evening. She had to be efficient and polite to all the customers and although she managed both, it was a strain – there was no doubting that. Afterwards, with her work finished for the day, there was the shopping to be done on the way home, keeping an eye open for bargains to make sure the bill didn't come to more than our budget could cope with. There was, after all, no sense in throwing money around. Every penny counted, didn't it?

The cold Essex wind was blowing outside as I handed her the glass of wine – an inexpensive brand, from our local supermarket – and we wandered into the vast living room where we had made love so often in the past in front of the crackling log fire. Like lovers the world over, we began to talk about the events of the day.

I had only known Lisa a comparatively short time, a matter of a few months, yet as I looked at her I knew more than ever that this was the woman I loved. I wanted her to share my life and I had told her so. There was one other thing I wanted to tell her too, a secret I knew in my heart of hearts I had to share with her.

No, it wasn't another woman. It wasn't gambling debts or a drink problem. There wasn't a skeleton in my cupboard that she didn't know about. There was no great embarrassment, either physically and mentally, that I had locked away; no shameful secret that would result in my beloved Lisa packing her bags on the spot and heading for the door at top speed. Yet there was certainly a 'secret' of mine I couldn't talk about that night, or any other night, come to that. Not just yet, anyway.

How could I explain that the rambling, oak-beamed home

we lived in wasn't, as I had told her, a friend's; or that I wasn't simply 'looking after the place for a mate', as I had said? Or that in hiding behind the padlocked garage door were luxury cars worth over £100,000 that I dared not let her see? Or that my family and friends were sworn to keep poor Lisa in the dark about my dreaded shame: I was rich. Very rich.

Not just 'comfortable' or 'well off'. Not 'worth a bob or two' or 'doesn't need to work again' wealthy. Not even 'rolling in it' money. I was high-rolling, expense-no-object, wallet-busting, push-the-boat-out, the-drinks-are-on-me rich. I was, or had been – and to this day I'm still embarrassed to admit it – also 'more-money-than-sense' rich in that I'd left my brain outside the doors of the bank on certain occasions, especially when there was a pretty face in the vicinity, and watched as a chunk of my money disappeared. And that was why I was keeping my silence over the £10 million – yes, £10 million – that had arrived out of the blue one Saturday night courtesy of the National Lottery and changed forever the life of yours truly, a middle-aged working-class man from north London.

I had already blown part of my fortune on wine, women and song – and then more women – so now I was determined that the cash-in-the-bank factor wasn't going to destroy this new love, or influence it in any way.

I loved Lisa – I knew that. There was no doubt, no second thoughts, no hesitation. It was head-over-heels, misty-eyed, Mills and Boon stuff. I had fallen in love with her literally from the first moment I had seen her, Every time she brought my £1.99 full English breakfast to the table at her café, where I had become an habitué, and laid the steaming hot plate of early-morning bacon, egg, beans, sausage, fried bread and a mug of tea in front of me, I knew it with even more certainty.

But if I told her that I could afford to buy one hundred breakfasts every day of the year, or even the café itself, how would she react? Would the millions I had in the bank change the way she felt for me? Would it make her love grow or would it, with the twisted logic that money brings, ruin it all? I knew my fortune might bring even greater happiness to the love I felt we were destined to share – but it could also rip it apart.

As we sat down and began to eat that minted-lamb dinner, as the wind battered against the windows in that rambling old country house, I wondered once again how it had all started. How indeed…

1
War Baby

You'd have thought that in 1945 Adolf Hitler would have had more important things on his mind than trying to kill me.

I was spending most of my time in a cot, which wasn't too surprising given that I was only a few weeks old, so I wasn't really in a position to alter the course of the war anyway. Still, the Führer was never one for letting little details like that get in his way, and with Germany losing the war at a great rate of knots, in desperation he threw his last roll of the dice – the V2 bombs. Over 3,000 of them – the first man-made objects to be launched into space and the direct forerunner of today's space rockets – were launched against the Allies, and London was one of the prime targets for the Germans.

An estimated 7,000 people died as these killers haphazardly exploded in Britain and the Continent, and there could easily have been one more – me – had I lived a few doors away. Just down the road from our small house a silent-but-deadly V2 exploded that early spring day causing devastation and loss of life all around, but leaving me unscathed in spite of the shattered glass and débris that sprayed over me and my cot. Once all the commotion had died down, I was ready to get back to my baby sleep. Perhaps, just perhaps, it was the first sign that Lady Luck was going to smile on me in a way that defies logic even all these years later. It was the first time that I was to triumph over tragedy, but it certainly wasn't going to be the last.

In a fanciful way, it could also have been the Germans' way of getting back at the Johnson family, as my father had seen action against them in the First World War. After joining up (even though he was under-age), he served in the Royal Horse Artillery as a leading rider, pulling cannons into battle by six horses – yes, it was that long ago – and was one of the few who survived all the conflict from 1914 to 1918. During the course of the war, he even picked up four medals for bravery and service, and he must have deserved them all given that part of the carnage he survived was the Battle of the Somme – one million other soldiers didn't. On the first day alone, almost 20,000 British troops died – the worst day in our military history – but Dad got out in one piece.

Perhaps that was why that V2 fell near me – maybe Hitler was trying to get his revenge by wiping our neighbourhood, Edmonton in north London, off the map. That is the only reason I can think of. Either that or the rocket got 'lost' on its way to a more prestigious destination than the area where I was born and bred.

I'm not knocking Edmonton, far from it, but let's be honest, it's hardly the most salubrious part of town. In the ninth century the Vikings had managed to sail up the River Lea, which runs through the area, but not too many people followed in their footsteps in the years to come as shortly afterwards the encroaching marshland made it hard for any big boats to get through. Even the New River that runs through it isn't all that new – it dates back to Tudor times. And it's not even a river, just a channel cut from the River Lea in an attempt to bring fresh drinking water into poor old London town all of 400 years ago.

Nowadays, Edmonton is probably best known as a turning off the busy A406, the North Circular Road, and for its massive IKEA showroom, famous for its opening-night chaos when 6,000 people rioted and one man was stabbed in the fight for the so-called bargains. It certainly wasn't, as they say, like that in my day. Riots were few and far between back then ...

Probably the most famous of all Edmonton's sons is Bruce Forsyth, the game-show host and one of the few people who can genuinely be called a 'showbiz legend'. Bruce, whose family were garage-owning Salvation Army members, went to our most famous local school, the Latymer School, and was already busy working as a 15-year-old with a song, dance and accordion act called 'Boy Bruce, the Mighty Atom' when I entered the world on 26 January 1945.

I was born at our three-bedroom council home – the one Hitler just managed to miss – in Montagu Road, not too far from Edmonton's reservoir and the massive sewage works alongside it. When I started looking into my family history in later life, I discovered that some of my ancestors had a pretty rough time too. Worst of all was my grandfather, who was killed in a robbery. My dad was only two at the time and his dad, my grandfather, was mugged in north London in 1898 for a gold watch he had on him. Everyone seems to think that mugging is a modern crime, but this took place when Queen Victoria was on the throne, for goodness sake, a period when everything was meant to be rosy in the garden and we could all walk the streets in safety. That might be the popular image, but what happened to granddad proved otherwise. At least one thing has changed: in this day and age you are lucky to catch anyone who commits a crime. Back then, they did at least catch the three men who attacked him. They were jailed, and even though they were only convicted of manslaughter, as far as I'm concerned they literally got away with murder.

My father, John 'Jack' Johnson, was a true gypsy, a Romany, a rag-and-bone man with Scots' blood running through his veins, and a man with a heart of gold who had been brought up in the Church of England faith. My mother, Louisa, was born in 1902 and brought up in the notorious Naranka Road on the borders of Edmonton and Tottenham. Her maiden name was Napier; she was of Irish descent and a Roman Catholic. It was still a marriage made in heaven, though, when they got married at Edmonton Register Office in the early 1920s, and their different backgrounds didn't seem to bother them one little bit. I have never met a couple so much in love as Mum and Dad. If any proof were needed of their love for each other, the nine children they had between them were there for all to see.

Mum had six children – one every eighteen months, in effect – and then took a rest. Well, she deserved it. Then three more came along and I was one of the second 'batch', the youngest of the lot. My mother, who was in her forties by then, had pneumonia around the time I was born and was in the North Middlesex Hospital for three weeks, so I had to be looked after by my elder sister, Mary, who was 22 years older than me. In fact, she was the one who changed my first nappy. So I grew up in this massive family with four brothers and four sisters and having them around all the time I felt protected.

Dad rented a Steptoe-like yard in Brettenham Road, east Edmonton, five or so minutes' walk from our house. He had a horse stabled there that would pull his cart around on its rounds, quite often in the Chingford area, which wasn't too far away. There were some other horses stabled in the yard – the coalman would keep his there too.

It wasn't just during the war that dad showed his courage; he was a bit of a hero in civvy street too a long time before I came on the scene. When he was a young man, he rescued a lad by the name of Smith, who had fallen in some water filled with toxic waste on an industrial dumping site near where we were brought up. In those days they didn't have the health and safety regulations we have now, so a heavy industrial area like north London had loads of dangerous places such as that which were fairly easy to get at, especially for inquisitive youngsters.

Dad didn't think twice about the risks he faced – I suppose

that after the battlefields of the war he was pretty immune to such thoughts – and he managed to pull the boy to safety, although the lad was scarred for life. Still, he probably would have died if it wasn't for dad's actions, so my old man really was a lifesaver. It's a great shame that my father – and especially my mother – never lived to see their youngest in the money.

It was a happy household, and having all those brothers and sisters around made me feel protected, in a way. Even today, all these years later, in my mind's eye I can still see Dad sitting by the open fire and lighting his pipe with a red-hot poker. You don't see many pokers in use these days – come to think of it, you don't see all that many pipes either.

I had a really good upbringing and we never went without. We had a good name and we all looked alike; wherever we went people would say to us, 'You're a Johnson, aren't you?' It wasn't a tough neighbourhood as such; it was very open – you could leave your door open without fear of burglars, and everyone helped each other out.

Dad earned a good living with his rag-and-bone business and he would even have an antiques dealer come round from time to time. He would put out all the decent clothes he had collected and prams and other stuff that he had repaired, put them out in our front garden and people would come round and buy them.

He had a couple of garden sheds at the back of the house and filled them with all sorts of stuff – wirelesses, wind-up record players, old 78 records, anything really. We were very into toy soldiers when I was a boy, and I remember once he went to this factory and brought home three sacks of lead toy soldiers. He gave us a dozen each and melted the rest down for the lead. They don't make them out of lead these days, so they would have been really collectable, had we kept them. The amount of stuff that my father brought home over the years would have made the money I was to come into in later life look like a drop in the ocean.

Dad was a little man but very strong; I saw him lift whole gas stoves and carry them on his back. My mother was a big woman and she had a pinafore that she would always wrap around her; she looked like one of those big 'mommas' that you see in Tom and Jerry cartoons. She loved all the children, though being the youngest I was spoilt. My brothers and sisters used to give me sixpence each or, if there was no money, they would give me chocolate instead.

I remember when I was four or five we went on holiday, hop-picking in Kent. We would go on Dad's cart, which was covered, a bit like the old television Western *Wagon Train*, and we went in this three-strong convoy over Tower Bridge on our way to Kent. It took us two days to get there. Mum and Dad were up front and I was with two others in the back. The rest of the family would be in the other carts.

Everyone got paid, even the kids, and we stayed in a chalet – a wooden hut, really, with a communal outside toilet – for two weeks. But it was our holiday because we were out in the fresh air all that time.

Apart from that, our only other holidays were visits to my brother, who had been stationed in Lancashire during the war and married a Lancashire lass; we'd catch a coach from Victoria and visit him in Wigan. From there we'd go to Blackpool or Southport for a day out, and we also made a few trips to Liverpool.

My sister had married a coalminer and we'd get the train from King's Cross to visit them in Durham. It was a typical miner's terraced home, the sort familiar from *Coronation Street*, and my brother-in-law would come home as black as the Ace of Spades and wash in the tin bath in front of the fire.

There were antiques everywhere around our home from Dad's work. Sometimes, when I was small, he used to take me out with him on his rounds. We might stop off for tea and cakes or something; I loved that, because I was fond of sweet things back in those days. I remember lying on the back of the cart on top of all these clothes and rags and you could detect this horse smell. I'm not being rude about Dad, but somehow that smell stayed with him all the time, even when he wasn't doing his rounds, no matter how much he washed. He also bought packets of ten 'Weights' cigarettes at a time and saved the ends of them in a little tin. Then, at night, in front of the fire, he'd gather all the tobacco together and roll it into a cigarette paper while the poker was resting in the burning fire. When he'd finished he'd take the now red-hot poker and light his home-made cigarette with it.

After going to Brettenham Road Infants School, I moved on to Montagu Road Secondary Modern when I was 11, just the same as the rest of my brothers and sisters. I didn't love school and I didn't hate it – 'medium' is my verdict on it. I was good at cricket and art, but that's about it; I didn't shine in any other subjects. All the children in the family would make home-made holly wreaths, which we could sell for about 5 shillings (that's 25p) each.

Dad died of a heart attack when I was 14 and he was 69. He hadn't been ill at all and it came as a shock to everyone. I was camping with some friends at Cheshunt and came home on the Sunday to be told it had all happened on the Saturday. Dad only used to work half a day on a Saturday; apparently, he came home, had a pain in his chest and that was that. I think he died in the ambulance on the way to hospital.

He hadn't talked much about his Romany ancestry, but my mother told me all about it, and at his funeral literally hundreds of people turned up, all dressed in black. It looked like a Mafia funeral. They had come from all over the place, though after the funeral they disappeared and we never saw any of them again.

I lost my virginity when I was 14 to a very nice girl called Christine. It happened in our house when Mum was away on a day-trip to Whipsnade Zoo. Unfortunately, it rained a lot, so she came home early – just in time to see me and Christine coming out of the house together – and she immediately put two and two together.

I left school when I was 15 and of course things were tough: Dad was the breadwinner, after all, and now he was gone.

The family rallied round to help Mum, but Dad hadn't left her anything really and she was still devastated at losing him. I drew closer to her because of her loss and would help out with the chores, chopping wood for the open fire that we had and things like that. She didn't have to go out to work but eventually she did, working around the North Circular Road at Chingford at the London Rubber Company – the condom makers – part-time in the canteen.

Obviously I had to get a job. I had three brothers and a brother-in-law who worked at Allen and Greaves Engineers on an estate in Edmonton and I got a job there as an apprentice. They made fire-proof doors and I was paid the princely sum of £3 a week plus a bonus of £1 to £1.50 every fortnight depending on how well the company was doing. I would give my mother £2 a week and I'd have £1 left to paint the town red!

Still, I managed to buy my first suit, a lovely Prince-of-Wales check that I bought off the tallyman who was selling suits door-to-door. I paid off at about one shilling a week and I can't for the life of me remember how much it cost in total, but it took an eternity to pay for it. And it was about twenty times too big for me, but the man selling it persuaded me it fitted perfectly and I fell hook, line and sinker for his sales pitch.

After father died, I started to go out. By the time I was 16 I was earning money. I don't drink much now but in those days I'd drink brown and mild or light and bitter. (There's a couple of drinks you don't hear much about these days!) A bit later on in the night I moved on to lager and then vodka or whisky mac. I'd come home paralytic. Best of all, around Edmonton there were loads of bands who would appear at the pubs and I'd go to places like The Angel, The Horse and Groom or The King's Head to see the band and have a drink and a dance. A typical Friday night for me would be watching *Ready Steady Go!* on television while I was getting ready and then I'd head on out to The King's Head and hopefully then on to a party somewhere.

I was a bit of a rocker at one stage and when I was 17 I passed my bike test and bought a 250BSA motorbike. I'd leave it outside my home at night and, just to show how long ago this was, I didn't even need to lock it up. No one would steal a bike from outside your house, after all, would they? I used to go to a famous rockers' café called The Ace Café on the North Circular Road; my little bike looked like a kid's cycle next to some of the machines there. I would be in my leather jacket and we'd all hang around having coffee and looking at each other's bikes. It was like a scene out of *Grease*.

But then I got bored with being a rocker and decided to become a mod. I bought a Lambretta – I wanted a Vespa, but the Lambretta was cheaper – and had a fox's tail on the back aerial and corks from wine bottles on the wing mirrors. I'd ride around with my fur-hooded parka on to keep warm and underneath I'd have a suit on – that meant you could pick up a young lady and put her on the back of the scooter in a way that you couldn't on the back of a motorbike.

We'd go up the East End, to Roman Road, where there'd

be pubs and action, music and girls. There wasn't much in the way of drug-taking, not like today. I did try some 'blues' – little tablets to get you going – but they never did anything for me. I just loved the music and the atmosphere – and the drink.

My mod days lasted for a little while. I remember once having a punch-up in Brighton with the rockers and ending up with a bloody nose, so I high-tailed it out of there.

Soon I bought my first car, a blue Morris Mini for £350 on hire purchase and although it was only a few months old I could afford it, thanks to the h.p.

The Beatles were just exploding on the scene at the time, so I went to John Collier, 'the Window to Watch', and bought myself a Beatle-style suit in black with cloth buttons and a red lining to the jacket. I had my winkle picker shoes, too, which we'd buy from Edmonton Market. We also went to Walthamstow Market and, if we'd got some money, we'd go to the King's Road to buy that one 'special item', whatever that might be that particular week. I had a little cardboard handkerchief with zig-zag material at the top to go in the breast pocket. It looked smart, but if a woman was in distress it wasn't very good for helping her dry her eyes!

Once I'd got the Mini I used to work my socks off and then every Friday night I'd get in the car with some mates who'd help to chip in for the petrol and head off up north to The Cavern in Liverpool. I'd stay at my brother's in Wigan and he'd put my mates up too. We'd actually seen The Beatles there before they became famous, before they even went to

Hamburg. And there were also great bands such as Gerry and the Pacemakers and Billy J. Kramer and the Dakotas – who to this day are one of my favourites – on there.

We used to go on a boat – the ferry across the Mersey, called *The Royal Iris* – to hear the bands who were playing. In Liverpool, the birds we used to get hold of … We were all good-looking lads and we had the Beatle hairstyles, so we'd take the girls we met into the car or behind the back of a building or whatever. It's embarrassing to talk about it now, but it was all normal behaviour really. The girls all loved us to bits and they'd always have a relative in London and they'd mention the road the relative lived in and expect us to know it – they didn't seem to realise just how big London was.

One of my friends – a lovely man, who had a hair-lip – and I decided we could cash in on this music, so I bought an old Grundig tape recorder and a guitar. We couldn't play and we couldn't sing but we recorded ourselves doing 'She Loves You' with my mate with the dodgy lip singing. It sounded terrible.

Later on in the Sixties, for a very short period of time – perhaps just weeks – I became a hippy. I grew my hair and wore a band around my head and put on a kaftan. We'd go down to Southend beach and tell strangers to 'make love not war'.

By the mid-Sixties I was in my early twenties and still working at the engineering factory. There was a lad working there whom I befriended and one day he took me round to his home in Edmonton to meet his mother and father – and his sister. I met the sister, Gloria Glass, and I was immediately besotted with her; we made a beeline straight for each other. The trouble was, she was engaged and had been going out with her fiancé for four years before I came on the scene.

Her mother and father – he was a window cleaner (yes, called Glass!) – did not approve of me. After all, they had known the other chap for four years. The father told me not to see her any more but that did not stop us. In the end, we ran away to my brother's in Wigan and stayed in his spare room because we wanted to be together so badly. I got a job in an engineering factory up there, because it was what I was accustomed to, and she got a job working for Kay's Catalogues.

Her father had search parties out looking for her, which was quite natural really, and our next move was going to be to go to Gretna Green to get married. But while we were in Wigan she got appendicitis and that meant the hospital had to get hold of her next of kin, the parents, and notify them about her.

I had to ring her parents and they came up to see her: the father, the mother and an uncle. They told us, 'Okay, if you love each other that much, get engaged and wait for three or four years before getting married.' But we didn't want to wait that long. She got pregnant – we planned it, we didn't want to wait for years. As soon as it happened, we got married at the Register Office in Edmonton. By this time we all understood each other and the parents were okay at the wedding.

We lived with Gloria's parents for a couple of months but then my mother invited us to come and live with her in the house where I'd been born. Our son, Nicholas, was born in 1967 and then we got a brand-new council flat, twenty storeys in the air near Edmonton Green, right near where Bruce Forsyth's dad had his garage in Victoria Road.

Life was all right in one sense, but then it started to get a bit hairy because Gloria started to think about the guy she had been engaged to for four-and-a-half years. It didn't help that her mother was saying she should have married him! But I wanted it all to be hunky-dory, especially with us having a son.

A year after Nicholas, we had a daughter, Tina, and we also moved home. One night, however, I had a terrible nightmare that the kids had fallen out of the tower block so we moved back to Montagu Road, to a three-bedroom maisonette. And that is when the trouble really started …

2
Hard Times

We were doing all right. I had a job working on a production line making mains gas appliances. Then Gloria decided she wanted to work too, so she got a job at a mini-cab firm as one of the telephone controllers. You can imagine what it was like, all the guys would be there waiting for their next job and they would be chatting her up in between. It ended with her having an affair with one of the drivers – someone who reminded her of the man she had been engaged to, as a matter of fact.

I didn't know anything until she told me about it. Then she just upped and left me alone to care for our two young children; he left his two boys too. I didn't know what to make of it all. I was devastated, in a terrible state. All I could do now was do my best to look out for the two children, Nick and Tina. I carried on working but I could not cope. My mother helped by looking after them but I was getting calls all the time at work telling me to come home because there was this problem or that problem with the children.

I remember the first time that I took Nick to school on my own, the same school I had been to as a youngster. Nick became almost a recluse, only talking to me and my mother. He'd talk to the other kids in class sometimes, but only a little bit. He's all right now, of course, but it really did hit him as a little lad, much more than Tina.

If Gloria had taken the two kids it would have been tough enough, but she left them with me. She did not even get in touch with them for months. Then, one day, there was a knock on the door and I heard her saying to one of the children, 'I have got a lot making up to do with Daddy.' I think she lasted two days and then she was off again. This time I didn't see her for years. During those two days I told her I was willing to have her back for the sake of the kids and that these things happen. But then she told me she couldn't hack it and went back to the other guy again; I think she went off with him to Doncaster for a while. I didn't see her for three or four years after that.

In those days it was unusual for the father to have custody of the children. I remember that I had to go to court and get legal custody of them and once that happened it made me feel really, really secure. The love I had for those children was immense but I must have had some psychological help from someone up there looking down on me. Looking back, I don't know how I coped; I have not got a clue. I was not even working and was surviving on social security.

There were no cards from her for the kids on birthdays or at Christmas; I suppose he had left his children and she didn't want his and he didn't want mine. But she knew that I could manage, and that is what I did. I used to do a bit of labouring work for a builder and he paid me £5 a day cash in hand, which helped me out a bit – but he wanted his pound of flesh, I can tell you.

I thought I needed a fresh start so I got a council exchange and me and the kids – who were really beautiful by this time – moved out to Ponders End, near Enfield. On this estate where we lived there were a lot of single women too – in fact, it was known as Divorce Alley, and in the afternoon they would invite me round for coffee and a chat. One of them would show me how to make a particular meal and another would do some washing for me. I would look after their kids for them if they went out and vice versa. I was one of the divorcees, but a male version. Every other night I would sit on the stairs and sob my heart out. I was looking for a mother for the kids, I guess – I used to talk to all the girls about it and what I should do.

Eventually, I decided that I should go back to work and got a child-minder. She was quite well-to-do, actually, with two children of her own, and she looked after my kids when I started work in a very good job as a warehouse manager in Tottenham for a firm supplying kitchen furniture. Then she and I had an affair. We went out together to West End shows or for dinner. She was a very decent girl – I'll call her Clare – and it was all a bit like *The Brady Bunch* with me, her and the four children who were all about the same age. I was divorced by now and so was she, but I just didn't feel it was going anywhere. She knew that too, so she called it a day, and that was a bit like a kick in the teeth, but it was too late by then for anything to happen so we parted.

I had quite a few affairs after that, but there was never anyone who was really suitable, bearing in mind that I was looking for someone to 'mother' my children too.

I love all my family to bits, don't get me wrong, but not many of them helped me in those days. I think their motto was 'You made your bed, now lie in it' and so they didn't get involved – with the exception of my elder brother Danny and his wife Stella, who did look after the kids at times.

Although I was a bit of a man about town, my first priority was the kids. I didn't know where Gloria was and I never heard from her at all – I've no idea what she was feeling inside. I was thinking of the kids all the time and I was trying to do my best, but one time I had to go to social services in Enfield and confess, 'As much as I love my kids, I can't handle this.' I got a call from them the next day asking, 'Are you all right, Mr Johnson?' and I told them I was. They knew I had just been going through a bad phase and that I was all right again. It's a good job they appreciated that, because they could have taken the children away from me.

The meals I was cooking for the children were pretty basic, things like spaghetti Bolognese or shepherd's pie and sometimes I would go to the shop and buy a pound of 'pot herbs' as we called it – a potato, an onion, no meat – and make a stew out of that. Once I remember my daughter asking me, 'Where's yours, Dad?' I told her, 'I will get mine later when you are both in bed,' but really there was nothing left for me to eat at all. I never let on, though.

By this time I had learnt to wash, cook and clean, but the one thing I couldn't do was iron. I never got the hang of it. I used to take my daughter's school uniform and put it under the chair and sit on it to 'iron' it.

Then I met a guy I had known some years before. He was quite well off and he would bankroll me on nights out on the West End, going to restaurants and chatting up girls. Thinking about it now, perhaps he was using me on those nights out – he was married and he wanted a pal to go out on the town with.

My life was full of ups and downs though, to be honest, it was mainly downs. It was so draining in that I was thinking of the kids all the time and I just wanted the best for them. I'm no super-hero, but often I looked at them and thought to myself, 'If they haven't got me they haven't got anybody.'

At one stage my nephew, who was the same age as me, said he would look after the children for a couple of weeks. It turned out he was doing it for his own ends – he wanted to adopt them; he and his wife were having trouble having children of their own. I told him straight: 'I may not have much but no thank you: I love my kids and they are staying with me!'

I bought them second-hand bikes and we would go riding alongside the River Lea. My mother had moved to

Enfield and sometimes she would look after the children and feed them.

Then I met another woman. I was now divorced from Gloria, but my new woman was married; she had four children and I had two. Before long, she had left her husband and moved in with me. But then she became very religious and got involved with a group of people who told her that it was a sin for unmarried people to live together. I was not into the religion in the same way that she was, but in the end we both agreed that we should get married. We tied the knot at Edmonton Register Office and moved into larger accommodation at Palmers Green near the North Circular Road; shortly afterwards, our son Gavin – who is now known as Zak – was born.

But the marriage was a struggle, there is no disguising that, and even all these years later I find it painful to discuss my relationship with this woman – who I don't want to name – and her relationship with the children freely. We were together for about eight years before divorcing and eventually she found someone else. I was living back in Edmonton and first Tina, who was then 15, and Nick, who was 16 or 17 at the time and at college, moved back in with me in the three-bedroom maisonette. We had an option to buy and so when the children were a little bit older and earning money, we did. Tina met her husband-to-be (they are still married) and she moved out to a place in Tottenham and then out to North Weald in Essex; after living there for three years we sold the maisonette and Nick and his girlfriend moved out to North

Weald too and I moved into a little one-bedroom flat near them both. Meanwhile, Zak had left home and was living a student lifestyle in Hastings. I would go to see him once a month or so and take him food parcels and stuff like that.

By this time I was running three jobs: I was a door-to-door salesman for part of the night, a chauffeur in the day and in the evenings when I was free I was a mini-cab driver.

As a salesman, I found myself going door to door, cold-calling, trying to sell household products like cleaners and dusters; it was pretty soul-destroying, I can tell you. The chauffeuring was more interesting by a mile. At first I would just drive the mourners to and from the funerals, in either a Daimler or a black stretch limo. Then one of the guys got sick and I helped out in other areas. I had never seen a dead body in my life and the first time I was asked to move one I thought, 'I can't do that!' But I did.

The company liked me, I was good at my job, and they put me at Number One, the hearse driver. I did that for five years, for all sorts of funerals: Catholic, Protestant, Hindus, whatever. You could also pick up some useful overtime pay: you were given a bleeper and had access to a Mitsubishi ambulance to go and pick up dead bodies. I saw everything: people who had thrown themselves in front of trains, children, murder victims, suicides, everything. I even had to cut down people who had hanged themselves.

We picked up Police Constable Keith Blakelock, the officer who was stabbed to death in the Broadwater Farm riots in

Tottenham. I was paged on the Sunday night and we had to take him to Hornsey Mortuary. That poor man was well hacked about, I can tell you. We had to train the police on how to carry his coffin – we did it with a coffin filled with lead weights – and I eventually drove the hearse to his funeral service in Muswell Hill. I also drove the hearse that took the comedian Peter Sellers' body to Golders Green Crematorium in 1980 and helped carry the coffin into the building.

It wasn't all grim, though. I know it sounds a strange thing to say, but in many ways this was the funniest job I ever had in my whole life. There were a lot of young people working there, it was a large firm and we all used to have a good laugh whenever we could. It was all part of a defence mechanism too, as you needed to smile otherwise things would have become very morbid.

Sometimes I'd be driving at three or four funerals a day. As the cortège travelled slowly through the cemetery I'd look at all the headstones to read the inscriptions and epithets on them. Once, when it had been snowing and the ground was covered in snow and ice, I found myself looking at the writing on the stones with about twenty cars behind me in the procession as we went slowly through the cemetery with the funeral director walking in front of me in his hat and tailcoat. When I looked back to the front of the car again, he had disappeared. I thought I'd better brake, so I slammed to a halt and the first thing I saw was this hand coming over the bonnet of the hearse. He'd slipped and gone to ground and I just managed to stop before going over him! He needed to grab the bonnet to pull himself back on his feet and carry on with the funeral.

Obviously, part of the job was to carry a coffin from the hearse to the grave. If it was a family plot, the mourners would all gather round on the rocks or under the trees and move aside while we negotiated our way to the graveside. On one occasion, one of the family mourners was under a tree and when he moved a little his wig got caught in the branches of the tree; as he moved off the wig remained there, hanging from the branch. The coffin was shaking by the time we started to lower it into the ground as we were all laughing so much. At other times we found that the gravedigger had made the hole too small for the coffin to fit into, so we'd have to put our feet on it and gently try and ease it in with all the mourners standing by looking on.

One incident almost got me the sack. On Sundays we would sometimes handle Jewish funerals and the rabbi who was officiating would sit in the hearse alongside me when I was driving. On this occasion we arrived at a house about five minutes early so the rabbi told me, 'Don't stop, just pull up round the corner for a few minutes.' So that's what I did. But you could see into the house and I could see the wife and the daughter of the dead man laughing away. Then we went back at the time we were due and the couple came down the steps outside the house screaming and wailing.

The rabbi told me to go round to the back of the hearse and open the door. The mother and the daughter clutched the coffin and said, 'Speak to me, speak to me.' Well, I don't know what came over me – possibly the sight of them giggling away had got to me. Anyway, I said to them, 'I'm all right, are you all right?' The mother and daughter didn't say anything, they took it okay really, but I got a severe telling-off for that.

You'd get to know all the vicars and priests in that line of work. They're all hypocrites, if you ask me. I'd be taking them to the funeral and they'd ask for the name of the deceased as they had forgotten it. Yet at the service they'd be talking about them as if they'd been friends for fifty years or more. Some of them would fall asleep in the hearse; some of them would pass wind on the way to the funeral. One of the vicars used to arrive on a little scooter and leave his crash helmet outside with it. So the lads would put pine cones in there for when he came back and tried to put it on.

In the funeral parlour at Edmonton the chauffeurs' room was next to the mortuary. Some of the guys would get a piece of string and tie it to the hand or wrist of one of the bodies in there and then run it over the top of the door. Whenever you got a new chauffeur or one who was visiting, you'd ask them if they wanted a cup of tea and they would say 'yes' so you'd send them into the next room to get a cup or mug. As they opened the door they'd walk into the room and the arm of one of the bodies would lift up, pulled by the string. You never saw anyone move so fast as the guys who saw this dead arm being raised to greet them!

Sometimes I'd want to meet Tina and take her for lunch or something. But I'd want to pick her up from the lawyers' office in Wood Green where she was working, so I'd arrive in the hearse. She refused to get in it with me – I guess you can't blame her really.

All in all, I was at the undertakers for about seven years and I was earning about £20,000 a year with the other jobs. But it does get to you after a while, working at a funeral place, plus I had to change jobs anyway as I wanted to move out to Essex to be near the kids. So then I got a job with a printing company at Harlow – Seri-Graphics – who were a big organisation that did work for companies such as Tesco. All the brochures and the 'buy one, get one free' leaflets would be done by us. I did a bit of everything really, helping out on the machines, the packing and so on. I did a lot of driving too, going up and down the country delivering and making sure everything got to the right place. I was 47 when I started work there and 53 when I left. I was living in a beautiful maisonette at the time, a one-bedroom place in Cunningham Rise in North Weald.

I didn't have a lady in my life at the time (my only companion was my black Labrador, Marcus) – perhaps partly because of the problems I had had before, but also because I was simply too busy. It was work, come home, go to bed; work, come home, go to bed. It just went on like that. By the time Saturday came around I would be absolutely shattered.

Tina and Nick would ask me round for dinner on occasions, but I'd have to fend for myself the rest of the week, so on a Saturday I'd make three or four dinners – shepherd's pie or spaghetti Bolognese – freeze them and put them in the oven when I wanted them to save having to cook every night.

Round the corner at North Weald Market there was a bloke who would sell knock-down meat that was only just in date, so was going cheap. Once I bought ten airline dinners for £2 off him. I went home and sat in the chair eating from this plastic tray with one roast potato in and some meat in the next dish and a sweet in another dish, imagining that I was actually flying on the way to some exotic Far Eastern country. It was hilarious to me at the time, but seems rather sad too, looking back now. The only social life I had was when I would go out with my son or daughter; their friends were my friends, as it were, because I did not have anybody else up there. I didn't go out for a drink on my own or anything like that – I was virtually a recluse.

My pride and joy was my second-hand blue MGM Midget and even in winter I would drive around with the top down, wrapped up in a flying jacket to keep me warm. My main hobby at the time was going to car boot sales and I would snap up any music videos I found there, especially Eric Clapton, Gloria Estefan, The Beatles and Elton John.

I have always thought of myself as a jovial figure who could make people laugh, but back then, underneath, I wasn't a happy bunny at all. There I was, in my early fifties, living in a small flat all alone and that seemed to be that. This was all life had in store for me.

3

Ticket to a New Life

The National Lottery had not been out for long and just like everyone else, I started playing it. I'd spend £2 a week on a couple of lines of numbers and I even won the odd tenner here and there. When I first started I would select the numbers carefully and then sit there on a Saturday night checking them. If I did not win I would go to bed early in a furious mood.

But in my heart I knew I was going to win something. I believe what goes round comes round. I had had so many bad knocks I just felt that it was time something good happened to me, something *really* good. And boy, was I right ...

There was a time when I did the Lottery and used the same numbers every week based on numbers that were special to me; it's the sort of system a lot of people use. Children's birthdays obviously formed part of it, and so did the numbers one and seven. I don't want to go into too much detail about my beliefs here, but I believe there is one creator and the number seven also appears several times in the Bible, so those numbers would be used too whenever I entered the contest. But I did do the Lottery every week without fail and one thought kept crossing my mind: if I always used the same numbers and forgot to enter one weekend and the numbers I always selected came up as winners then it would be more than I could stand. So I decided to do random numbers instead, changing every week – a lucky dip, so to speak. That way, if I missed a draw because I hadn't got a ticket then I'd have no idea whether I would have won or not. When I did buy a ticket it was only one week at a time; I didn't do a batch of several weeks in advance like some people. I did this for about a year; two choices every Saturday, none on a Wednesday. That way I'd be spending £2 a week and every now and then getting a tenner back for having three numbers. I never won more than that, though.

At the time, I was still working at the printers and it was quite demanding work. I'd done several '24 hours' with the shifts I was on and by the end of May 1998 I needed to get away, to be on my own. I also fancied getting a bit of a suntan, so I thought I'd go down to the beach in my old Ford Fiesta with my faithful dog Marcus. There was no particular work on offer that weekend, so I decided to go down to Hastings. My son Zak was studying down there, so I sort of knew the area, and I knew that Paul McCartney lived somewhere in the region of Rye and Hastings, but I didn't know much else about that part of the world. Looking back, I haven't got the faintest idea why I chose to go there in particular. I went to Millets in Harlow and bought a one-man tent for £14 and a little cooker. Then I got some pots and pans out of the kitchen at home and set off.

The weather looked promising and after getting down there, I spotted this site right by the beach that looked lovely. On the way I'd stopped and got some milk and a couple of eggs and food for the dog. I smoked, so I got some cigarettes too and the plan was to spend Friday night and Saturday night down there and head back on Sunday.

Zak was going out with a girl called Donna back then and her mother and father owned a caravan on a site, although I had no idea that it was the same site I was heading for. I paid my money to camp there for the weekend and no sooner had I got in than I bumped into Donna's parents. I wouldn't have planned to do things that way because I just wanted to be on my own and … well, to be honest, they were boring, frumpy people. They asked me if I wanted to join them but I said that I'd prefer to be alone, which was true. They insisted that I should come round on the Saturday night, though, and join them for a barbecue at their caravan. I was to pop in and the arrangement was that I'd get some meat to bring round for myself to cook on their barbecue.

That Friday night was to be the last night of my 'ordinary' life, though, of course, I'd no idea of that at the time. An average evening, in many ways, but I can still remember it in detail. By the time I'd got down to the site it was gone eight-thirty in the evening. I didn't have a toaster, so I couldn't even have toast. I had some bread and butter and some baked beans, but that didn't fill me up, so then I had some sardines out of a tin. If you are with someone you make an effort when it comes to what you eat, but I was on my own and so I just ate to fill myself up – I didn't really care what the 'menu' read like. I washed it all down with some tea and I had a large bottle of Sprite too in case I got thirsty. It wasn't a typical English night, it was actually quite nice, and so I rounded it off by going for a walk along the beach with my dog. On the Saturday morning Zak turned up with Donna and I took a stroll into Hastings town centre and went to Sainsburys to buy some meat for the barbie – a little piece of steak, as I'd decided to treat myself to a small fillet. I noticed the Lottery queue at the supermarket was quite empty so I thought I might as well get my ticket while I was there.

You could say that it was one of the best decisions of my life – and you'd be right. I remember asking for two Lucky Dips but I had only a solitary one-pound coin on me. The rest was all shrapnel – a load of two-pennies and one-penny pieces. I counted it out religiously to the woman behind the counter and it seemed to take a lifetime to get the second £1 together. By this time the Lottery queue was filling up pretty fast and there was a lot of tut-tutting behind me, people murmuring, 'Hurry up, I've got things to do!' I had my jeans on and when I got my ticket I shoved it in my back pocket. My first line of numbers was 7, 9, 13, 25, 32 and 47, chosen for me by the computer. The second line, the one that was to change my life forever, was 8, 20, 24, 35, 43 and 47. It was a rollover week and on the top of my ticket was the line 'Sat 23 May 98 – Guaranteed £20 Million Superdraw'.

One of the many punchlines in the comedy series *Little Britain* was 'The computer says "no".' When I bought my two Lucky Dip tickets and the computer chose the numbers for me it was very much a case of 'The computer says "yes".' And it was to say 'yes' in the most astonishing manner.

Nowadays I always put my Lottery ticket in my wallet because when the pager I carried went off later that crazy Saturday night telling me of the winning numbers I had to hunt around for my ticket. I never made that mistake again. That night I was larking about outside my tent, talking to Zak and his girlfriend Donna. I had a British Telecom pager on me that came from work – we had to have one in case we needed to be contacted. It was part of a system that was geared up to provide news flashes and it would also give out Lottery winning numbers on Saturday nights. The pager went off and displayed the winning numbers and little Donna started checking them for me.

We were actually in the tent at the time, me and Donna, and after the first three numbers came up, I was feeling pretty happy – I thought I'd won a tenner. Then the fourth number came up; I was amazed. But then the fifth number came up … and the sixth number! I thought somehow someone was having a laugh when they all came up – perhaps the guys at work were winding me up and had managed to send the numbers to me. Thinking back, of course, they wouldn't have known what numbers I'd chosen anyway, but thoughts like that run through your head at such times.

You could say I was quite excited. I had to find out whether I'd won for sure, though. Remember, this was before everyone had mobile phones and on this campsite there was just one public telephone. It was so 'ging gang gooly' that everyone was queuing up for it to ring home and tell their nearest and dearest what a lovely time they were having; I had to join the queue. Although I had a credit card on me I didn't have any coins to push in the box, so I had to phone my daughter Tina on a reverse-charge call. I remember hearing the operator tell her, 'There is a Mr Johnson on the line, will you accept the charges for the call?' Somewhat tersely, she accepted, greeting me with: 'Dad, what do you want?'

'Tina, I'm not sure,' I replied. 'I think I've won the Lottery.'

'You had better not be joking, Dad,' she told me, 'because I've just had a row with Kevin and I'm *so* wound up!'

'No, I'm sure,' I answered, 'I've got the numbers – I think I've won the Lottery.'

'Give me your numbers and I'll ring you back,' she told me.

I did and then put the phone down so other people could use it. By this time I was starting to pace up and down outside the telephone box and there was a queue outside the phone-box again as it was constantly in use. It rang. I knew it would be Tina, so I told the others in the queue, 'Excuse me, I have got to answer that call' and dived back into the box. It was indeed Tina and she said, 'Dad, give me those numbers again.' After I did she told me: 'Dad, take it easy. I have just phoned Camelot and there have been two winners – £10 million each!'

Can you imagine what went through my mind then? Can you even imagine? 'Tina, get down here quick,' I told her. 'I don't mind how you do it – helicopter, anything – just get down here and pick me up!' I was so excited I can't describe it. Then, all of a sudden, a fear dawned on me: I was walking around a strange camp site, I didn't really know anybody and in my back pocket was a ticket worth £10 million. I didn't know if anyone had heard the conversation – perhaps they had. All I know is that I went back to the tent and for some reason the only thing there was to drink was a bottle of Drambuie. So I drank the lot although somehow I didn't get drunk – I think it was because I was so excited.

Within about an hour or so two cars pulled up – Tina and my son Nick. We left the £14 tent there, one of the boys drove my Fiesta back and we went back to my daughter's house in North Weald. Nick looked very shocked by it all. He didn't look happy, in fact he didn't seem to know what was happening. You can't blame him. On the way back they'd phoned Camelot and told them, 'We think our dad's won the Lottery.' Camelot said the numbers seemed to be all right, they corresponded okay, but it was a Bank Holiday weekend and they couldn't check everything until the Tuesday. At this stage the only people who knew about the win were myself, my three children, Zak's girlfriend and his prospective in-laws and (perhaps) a few people on the site. It was impossible to keep it a complete secret, though. Everybody likes good news and even if you keep it to yourself initially, at some stage people are going to start to know.

We got back to Tina's about midnight. I could not sleep that night and neither could my daughter. I wanted to put the ticket somewhere. Bizarre as it sounds, she had an old oak drop-leaf table and I put the ticket for safekeeping between the legs. It was a big table and that was the only place I could think of. Every hour I would come down to check that it was safe. It was just for the one night and after that my daughter put it in a safe that she had in the house. On the Sunday morning we all went out as a family to have breakfast – nothing too fancy, just a Little Chef near Harlow. There was me, Tina and her husband, my brother's father-in-law, Zak and Donna, and Nick and his wife and children. All in all, there were about ten of us; we had breakfast, with tea and coffee, and I paid for it all.

I can't remember what else I did that Sunday, to tell the truth. I was mentally spending the money even then and my main thought was, 'How shall I look after my children?' I was staying at Tina's, in a normal ex-council-owned, three-bedroom house and just around the corner was my son's home, another former council house. I didn't make any more calls to Camelot. They had said that nothing could be done until Tuesday, so Sunday and Monday came and went. I didn't sleep at all either night because of all the excitement, but I wasn't tired one little bit as I was so energised by everything. I didn't go to Threshers or Oddbins and buy loads of champagne or anything like that, in case it was all a hoax or something went wrong. All the time, of course, I was thinking to myself that something was bound to have gone wrong. Perhaps there had been a mistake on the computer or something like that. I still had a nagging feeling that it might be a wind-up by the guys at work. Yes, I know it doesn't make sense as it would be impossible for them to do it, but odd things go through your mind at weird times like that weekend. I didn't really know why, but I had this sense that it was all too good to be true. Perhaps that's not an altogether unexpected feeling given the circumstances, come to think of it. At the same time you are thinking perhaps you should be at work on the Monday 'just in case' – you know, in case it all turned out to be a horrible mistake. But I didn't have to go in, I didn't need to work ever again. (In fact, it was to be over a month before I even turned up at work again, but more about that later.) It was like unloading 56lb of potatoes off my back: I felt free.

Sunday and Bank Holiday Monday came and went – the longest 48 hours of my life – and then it was the Tuesday morning. We were all round at my son's and at 9.30am there was a knock on the door. In came four men in suits, all of them carrying briefcases: two men from Camelot and two men from Drummonds Bank, the 300-year-old posh people's bank that is part of the Royal Bank of Scotland. I told them I wanted to keep the win quiet because I was worried about people coming out of the woodwork and to protect my children, and they were fine about that. If you want to keep it a secret they are with you 200 per cent of the way. But it was a bit like being treated as a prisoner to start with. They took pictures of me – front view, side views, pictures of my passport, driving licence, everything. I had to prove I was who I said I was. I didn't have my birth certificate, but my passport seemed to do the trick. Then they gave me the cheque! There was no waiting a few days or having to go to their office to collect it. There it was: 'Pay Joseph George Johnson' on Royal Bank of Scotland cheque number 196282. In the column marked 'tens of millions' there was the word 'one' and after that, in the remaining seven columns, the word 'zero'. In other words, exactly £10 million! Not the sort of cheque you get to handle every day. They told me that if I wanted to keep it all anonymous I shouldn't indulge in any large expenditure for a while. Of course, they were right. Not that I heeded their advice, mind …

Then the men from Drummonds said they had opened up an account for me. They explained how the win was tax-free but the interest I'd earn on the money wasn't and told me they'd come back in a couple of days with advice on things like PEPs and TESSAs. The group of them gave me a booklet called 'Out of the blue … it's You!', which they hand out to big winners. It had chapters in it such as 'Time to Start Planning' and 'Selecting Your Advisors', all that sort of stuff. The men talked to me about how much interest I would be earning from my win, but I didn't care; I *really* did not care. All I knew was that I was suddenly rich.

They had given me the cheque … and then, just before they went, they took it back off me! The reason was simple: they'd opened an account for me and it was best if they then paid the money in on my behalf – more secure for everyone. They did give me a copy of it, though, which I've kept to this day.

In the end, we wanted them to go. I know that sounds ungrateful, but it's not meant to be. It's simply that they'd been there for about three hours and we'd had enough; we just wanted to get on with things. After they left the house we were jumping for joy – we had won and that was that. First things first, time for a new car. My son-in-law Kevin knew all about cars so we decided I'd go out and buy one right away. My first thought was to get a two-seater BMW convertible and the next day we set off to Enfield to look for one. But soon we were at H R Owen, the upmarket car sales showroom in Hatfield, looking at Porsches.

We were both in jeans and looking scruffy as we scrutinised the cars, and the salesman approached us somewhat suspiciously. As soon as we said we'd be paying cash, however, his attitude changed straightaway. He even asked us if we'd like to smoke! I was determined to get a private number plate, decided on '223 Joe', and pretty soon it was on the car I'd bought on a banker's draft: a hard-top Porsche 911, for £70,000. By the Thursday or Friday it was mine and I drove back to my little maisonette from the showrooms with my foot down and the radio on full-blast. So much for not drawing attention to myself – there it was, this expensive new car parked outside my house! I spent the first night looking out through the curtains all the time just to make sure that it was all right. Over the next few days I'd just go out and drive around in the car for sheer pleasure. I wasn't going anywhere special, just out for a drive. I gave my Fiesta to my daughter-in-law's sister and I gave Donna my pager as a souvenir, as it was with her that I'd first checked my winning numbers. I also decided to treat everyone to a holiday. We would go to Florida on first-class flights, do all the sights and book four or five rooms at a luxury hotel.

There was only one problem: Donna's fear of flying. 'I've never flown before,' she told me, 'the plane might crash!'

I thought I'd reassure her. 'Donna,' I said, 'there's as much chance of the plane crashing as there is of me winning the Lottery!'

4

Not so Lucky

I hired rooms at a top-of-the-range hotel – the Dolphin, in Orlando. Tina and Kevin were great organisers and we hit Disney World, Epcot, WaterWorld, MGM and Universal Studios within days of landing. We overdosed on theme parks and I was shattered by the time it was finished. At the end of that we managed to get a break away from the queues in another part of Florida, but then it was time to come home and start spending a little bit of that £10 million.

I bought a Cartier watch for £10,000 for Zak and three white-gold 'love bangles' for Tina and my daughter-in-law for about £2,000 each. Cartier in Mayfair is like no other shop you have ever been in before. You sit in a wonderful comfortable armchair while deciding what to buy. I got to know the French manager there very well, as I went in so often! Even when I'd had nothing I'd always tried to save up for a smart T-shirt or something rather than get the cheap stuff, that's the kind of person I am. A little while earlier I'd been buying my clothes in charity shops; now I could afford to go to Gucci – so I did! On one trip to their Knightsbridge shop I spent about £1,000 on a lightweight jacket and I also bought some trousers and shoes. I spent £2,000 there that day and bought a handbag as a gift for £800. I'd constantly go to Harrods or Harvey Nichols with my daughter Tina to get some clothes or stuff for the kitchen. It's hard to say exactly what we purchased with the American Express card I'd decided to get, though, as things were happening so fast and we bought so many items.

Next, of course, we all needed somewhere to live. We saw some beautiful places in Essex but then we came across one we fell in love with about two miles away from where I had been living. Tilegate Farm at High Laver, near Ongar, was a seven-bedroom mansion with wrought-iron gates, a heated outdoor swimming pool, a tennis court, 13 acres of land and a large barn just opposite that we were to convert into another house, this time with six bedrooms. I bought it all from an East End boy-made-good for £1.3 million, paying half of the asking price myself with Nick and Tina each paying an equal portion of the other half from the amount I'd given them after my win.

Although I was only living in the annexe at the time I practically reinvented myself as lord of the manor – I got a Barbour jacket for £200, green Hunter wellies – the kind the aristocracy wear – for £100 and a shotgun with a licence for about £900. I had a new Range Rover to go with the Porsche, which cost me £40,000, and I 'inherited' some of the furniture too. I didn't need too much as I decided to live permanently in the annexe, but I did get a Bang and Olufsen sound system and a nice white leather sofa. We also 'inherited' Frank, the German gardener who lived in a little lodge next door. He's in his eighties now but still works harder than a man half his age. He was, and remains, remarkable.

We tried to keep my win secret. The only time I'd meet anyone who knew about me was if we bumped into someone when we went into the centre of Epping. But even then they didn't know exactly how much I'd won or what I was now worth. A lot of people knew about the win, but a lot more didn't. This may sound an obvious thing to say, but the reason I had not gone for publicity was primarily because I wanted to protect the privacy of my children. Also, I didn't want people coming out of the woodwork. I didn't want to be known as a Lottery winner either. When people asked me, 'What do you do?' I would reply, 'I'm an investor.' Well, that's not a lie, is it? I had invested £2 and won £10 million! Sometimes I'd say that I was in printing and had my own firm. It wasn't a total lie, really, as I had been a printer. Of course, I hadn't owned the firm, but I just didn't want everyone to put me in a drawer and label me 'Lottery Winner'.

I'd stopped working after 40 years of getting up and going to a job. I'd had that routine and suddenly, with the win, it all stopped. Now, some people find it difficult to adjust to that change, whether they've won the Lottery or retired, or been made redundant, or whatever. Me, I found it fantastic – no problem. Once, soon after winning the Lottery, I went past a street called Rays Road near Montagu Road in north London, where I'd been brought up. It was a little *Coronation Street*-style road with 60 or 70 small terraced houses on it. I remember thinking to myself, 'I could buy every house in that street if I wanted.'

I must say that Drummonds the bank were fantastic and they were investing the money for me in savings accounts such as ISAs and PEPs and as many Premium Bonds as it was tax-efficient to get – I think it was £30,000-worth for some reason, although I can't put an exact figure on it. The people from Drummonds would come every month to the house to see us for updates and eventually became friends of the family. They even invited us to a clay-pigeon shoot that they were holding. The Lottery people, Camelot, also asked me to a dinner and dance for all their big winners but I decided not to go as I had opted to remain anonymous and I thought it wouldn't be right for me to attend a very public sort of event. You read a lot about people who have won the Lottery, pissed it up against the wall and ended up skint. I wasn't going to do that. In fact a lot of people – both good and bad – have benefited from my win, as you'll see.

By this time it had been about a month since I'd won the Lottery and I still hadn't resigned from work – I just hadn't got round to it. I had mentioned my win to a couple of friends at work, though, so word must have got round a bit. Nevertheless, they were still all looking when I turned up a month after they last seen me dressed in casual gear – but now driving the Porsche, of course – to let them know officially that I wasn't coming back. The owners were all right, as were most of the guys there, and I wanted to leave on good terms – there was no reason to do it any other way. I certainly didn't go in with the intention of slagging anyone off, or being a show-off, or anything of that sort. Most people dream of what they will do at work if they ever get a big Lottery win – buy the firm, abuse the bosses, so on and so forth. I didn't feel like doing any of that; it wasn't my style. There was one of the managers, though – I won't name him, but he knows who he is – whom I told: 'I might buy the place and turn it into a pig farm!' He gave me a grin, but it was a really false grin, and he made out as if he'd enjoyed the joke. I don't think he was laughing inside, though. I could have taken them all for a drink, but they were at work. It was a normal working day for them: they couldn't drop everything and come down the pub with me, could they? So I left them to it.

If truth be told, even when I was working there I was living on my own and given the amount of hours I worked, I was virtually a recluse in a strange sort of way. There was one workmate I had there, not a massive mate, who was a shop foreman – I paid his mortgage off, that was £80,000. He and his wife couldn't have children, so I also paid for IVF treatment for them. He lived the other side of Harlow and a little while later, probably only a month or so after I'd paid off his mortgage, he phoned me up and asked if I could help him move because of the noise of all the planes coming into Stansted. Now, I got terribly hurt about that. I thought that was too much – I'd done enough for him, surely? In a way it was a little bit of a kick in the teeth. I didn't say 'no', I simply let it go.

My mother had died by the time I won the Lottery. That was a great shame, as it would have been wonderful to do something for her with all the money I'd suddenly got. She'd always said to me that I should look after my brothers and sisters, so I felt the obligation was there for me to give them some money. In a way, I felt bitter about it because, although I won't slag them off and they will always be welcome in my house, they had not been there for me and the children when things were rough all those years earlier. I do think they could have been more helpful than they were. Despite all that, with me behind the wheel of my new Porsche, my brother Danny and I went all up and down the country to members of the family, knocking on the door, staying for an hour and saying, 'There's ten grand,' 'There's ten grand,' 'There's ten grand'! We went to Margate, Basingstoke, Lancashire, all over the place. It made me feel much better; just because I had never had any help from them, that didn't mean that I'm like them. It made my conscience clear – and, to be frank, it didn't affect me too much financially as I was getting that back in interest on the millions anyway! I have a sister who is quite wealthy and she didn't need the money, but I still gave her ten grand. It was the same with all of them apart from Danny, to whom I gave £60,000.

One of the brothers, Charlie, was over the moon and was very grateful. He bought a few things for the house and I think he went on holiday to Scotland. He and Danny were more than grateful that I helped them out, but some of the others just accepted it as though it was a bit of chewing gum or something. One of my in-laws – again, I'm not going to mention any names – even phoned up other members of the family to complain that I hadn't given them enough. Well, if I was a ruthless Lottery winner and didn't care about anybody, I wouldn't have given my children £2 million each, would I? Yes, that's what I decided to give them. I think I was more than fair in what I did with everyone in my family. I didn't give my kids any advice on what to do with all that money; they were over 21 and old enough to know what they were doing with it. I did tell the youngest one, Zak, that it was a lot of money, though, and to be careful and be wise with it. (Mind you, he's now totally broke, so that turned out to be a bit of a waste of time!)

One thing was missing: I'd got all this money, the car, the house and everything, but I did not have a woman in my life at that time. I'd got a bit of catching up to do, so I phoned up an escort agency in the West End and asked them to send someone up to Essex to visit me. They asked if one was enough … or would I like two? I thought to myself: 'Why not? Let's go for it!', so two it was. You might laugh, but you want to do what you want to do, don't you? They came to my home – I was still living in the little maisonette – and asked me what I wanted. I didn't want to embarrass myself by giving any preferences, so I just said, 'Give me the full Monty' and believe you me, for two hours they did just that. They were two beautiful girls. One was from the North and one was a London girl. It cost me about £600 for the visit and I'd have paid twice that much. Talk about emptying your fuel tanks – that night lasted me for months! It's not something that I talk to people about generally, but it happened: it was part of my life at the time.

To be honest, I'm a hot-blooded man – I can't do without it. It's nothing to be ashamed of, is it? I thought about ringing the agency again but I didn't get round to it, so it stayed as a one-off.

Around this time, I decided to move out of Tilegate Farm. I was only there for a couple of months and it was all right at first living like the Brady Bunch, with me in my own quarters in the annexe, but eventually I wanted my own space. If I put my coat on, someone would ask, 'Where are you going?', and I didn't want to live in their pockets; I wanted a life of my own. It happened that the barn just opposite was being converted by us and so the council sent someone down to have a look at it. I was moving out of the house that day and had decided to do the moving myself, rather than use a removal firm. I was stripped to the waist and the boys, my son and son-in-law, were bringing my furniture out for me and I was stacking it into the back of the van I had got for the move. All of a sudden this council official with a handlebar moustache and tweed jacket, who'd come down to talk about the conversion of the barn, came up to me, poked his nose round the corner of the van and asked, 'Where's the owner?' I said,

'I think he's upstairs, can I help you?' and he said, rather rudely, 'No, you can't!' as though I was the scum of the earth. So I put him against the back of the van and told him, 'I *am* the owner – don't you talk to anyone like that!' He apologised quickly and off he went straightaway. That'll teach him to judge a book by its cover!

So, where was I off to? It was a place called Blackhall in a village called Moreton, near Ongar, not far from Tilegate, where my kids were now living. As soon as I saw it I'd fallen in love with it straightaway, no hesitation. It was 14th century in origin and at one stage had been used as a guildhall – the type of place where taxes were collected – with oak beams, a swimming pool, snooker table and three garages. Nearby were two pubs, The Nag's Head and The White Hart. It was on the market for £500,000, although it would be worth a lot more than that now. Before I bought it, I would drive past and imagine what it would be like to live there on my own. Would I be happy? Would I feel comfortable there? I decided I would be. The man I bought it off told me, 'Give me £500,000 and you can move in tomorrow' – and that's what I did. Nick and Tina gave me £500,000 for my share of the house I was leaving and I practically moved in the next day. I could even have bought a title to go with the house, one of those 'his lordship …' things you can get, but I decided not to.

When Zak first came to see Blackhall I thought I would play a little trick on him. He loves a joke himself and I knew he'd take it in good heart. I drove him to a cul-de-sac near to my real home, which was occupied entirely by old people's homes. I could see that he wasn't too impressed. I pointed to one in the corner and said, 'That's mine.' You should have seen the look on his face! He couldn't come up with anything more than 'Um …' I couldn't keep up the pretence for long, though. He knew he'd been had, but – as I knew he would – he saw the funny side of it. When he saw Blackhall he loved it and fell for it in the same way I had.

He wasn't the only one. It really was a gorgeous house, but as it was in the countryside ramblers or hikers would often pass by outside. Sometimes that would get on my nerves, so one day I decided to play a prank on them. A group of mainly middle-aged walkers paused outside, all togged up in their walking boots and carrying their plastic-coated ordnance survey maps. They stopped in the road, got out their cameras and started to focus on the house. I was so fed up with that kind of thing that I dropped my trousers and mooned at them through the window. Perhaps someone, somewhere, has a photograph of a millionaire's bare backside pressed against an ancient window. Not a pretty sight! Unfortunately, by an astonishing coincidence, one of the group happened to be my sister Grace, who is about twenty years older than me. My posterior wasn't anything she hadn't seen before, I guess, so she wouldn't be all that shocked. She certainly saw the funny side of it, as did the rest of the bunch, and didn't take offence. (I would like to point out that this wasn't something I made a habit of.)

I was determined that I would furnish the place in a style that was sympathetic with its 14th-century feel, and promptly

Above left: Mum and Dad at the seaside.

Above right: Mum, brother Danny and me, at home in Edmonton – the one that Hitler missed.

Below: The Johnson kids: Bill, Joanie, Charlie, me and Danny.

Above: Mum and me, aged about four, at Southend.

Below: (*front row*) nephew John (*left*) and me; (*back row*) brother Danny and a pal.

The swinging sixties. Me and my pal Johnny Whale, at a wedding (*above*) and out on the town (*below left*).

Below right: Many years later at another wedding. This time I'm giving away my daughter Tina.

The winning ticket (*above left*), the £10 million cheque (*below*) and the big winners guidebook they hand out to give a bit of advice on how to cope with it all (*above right*).

Above: Skydiving in Australia.

Below: Striking a posing after walking across Sydney Harbour Bridge.

My beloved Blackhall.

Lisa (*below*) and her boy Alfie (*above right*) once they'd moved into Blackhall with me. They had no idea about the millions at this time though; I'd even got rid of my cleaner to keep up the act!

Above left: The holiday from hell in Tenerife.

Above right: A kiss and a cuddle before Lisa heads off to the café.

Below: The £75,000 worth of 911 I kept in hiding.

set about doing so. There was a classy furniture shop in Brentwood in Essex and I bought a sofa there for more than £2,000. It was so wide and comfortable that when you put your bum on it, you practically disappeared! I bought a chair too, and that was so big that when I sat in it I was reminded of the comedian little Ronnie Corbett doing his monologues on the TV show *The Two Ronnies* in a huge chair that swamped him. Both the sofa and the chair were new, but I wanted to buy some antiques as well. I'd always enjoyed looking at antiques, but now I could buy as well as just look, so I'd go to the antique shops in and around Epping, looking for furniture that would go well with my new home. I bought a dark oak table, one of the kind so large that you have to shout to be heard by the person on the other side, and I picked up some matching oak chairs from another shop. The house had two massive open fireplaces, the type that you could actually sit in alongside the fire if you wanted, and to go with the general feel of the place my son Zak bought me a suit of armour that went in the hallway. I got reproduction swords that went up on the walls, some gladiator helmets, breast-plates and shields. We also had large, ornamental ceiling lights, the type of candelabras that cowboys used to swing on in the movies. It looked fabulous.

Everywhere I went I'd look for something suitable for the house. It wasn't long before antique dealers would start taking stuff round to my house for me to look at – bringing the mountain to Mohammed, so to speak. The White Hart pub was directly opposite where I lived and The Nag's Head was only a few yards away too. I got to know the owner of The White Hart well – he was a South African called Jim – and it got to the stage where I started to spend a lot of time there. He'd even call me up early in the morning to let me know there was breakfast for me if I wanted, and after eating that I'd go home and potter around for a bit and then go back to the pub at lunchtime. I'd have a few beers or lagers, but I've never been a really heavy drinker and even though I was spending a lot of time in the pub, the boozing didn't get out of hand. It was simply that I couldn't be bothered to cook – why should I? – so I'd go across the road for my meals rather than get busy in the kitchen at home. It also meant that I got to know a lot of the villagers as they came into the pub. One of the characters who would come in was a lovely old boy called John Webster; he'd been a bit of a ladies' man in his youth, from all accounts. Oddly enough, he once owned Blackhall. I'd greet him with a, 'Good morning, John, how are you?' and he'd answer in this beautiful, well-spoken voice, 'I'm bloody marvellous!' John was full of the joys of spring and he'd always have a couple of black Labradors with him, very well trained and behaved.

Talking of dogs, my own Marcus had come up in the world too, like me. Before I had my windfall I'd get him Tesco's own-brand food and mix it with something else. But afterwards Marcus had the best dog food there was, plus some fresh meat like chicken or mince at times too.

Blackhall wasn't fully furnished yet and I decided I needed some really nice, heavy curtains, the kind of thing that would fit in well with a house that was so old. I'd no way of knowing it, but that decision was to lead indirectly to one of the most eventful periods of my life. There was a local interior design shop run by two women, Mary and Eileen – not their real names, by the way – so I went there to look at the curtains they could supply. That visit led to them coming round to the house, measuring up and suggesting things that might be suitable. On another occasion, Mary came round on her own with some patterns for me to look at and I suggested we discuss it over lunch. You might be able to guess where all this ended up. I took her out in the Porsche for a bite to eat and then we went back to my home. The next thing we knew, we were making love. Soon, I took her round to meet the family as a 'friend'. Somehow I wanted her to be more than a friend, even though we were already sleeping together by this stage!

The two women thought it would be a good idea if they moved in next door to me while they were working on the house as there was a 'spare' building alongside me, a type of annexe, and they could use it as an office. Mary and Eileen had also bought a place in London's Docklands to rent out. I'd been thinking about buying a property somewhere in Chelsea, but they told me to come up and have a look at their place in the Docklands. Well, at this time there happened to be a penthouse for sale there at Sweden Gate in Baltic Quays and I loved it immediately. It overlooked the Thames and it had panoramic views and a spiral staircase that I was crazy about. I bought it, simple as that. It cost me £365,000, but I must have easily spent another £200,000 doing it up. Now, it might sound as though I was simply throwing money away here, but I wasn't. It was property, which is a good investment after all, and I do know the value of the pound, believe you me – or at least, I thought I did. I left Mary and Eileen to design it, telling them, 'Spare no expense.' I was in the position where I could say that and I wanted it done to the very best standards.

It cost me a lot, but it was fabulous at the end of it all. The light coming in was fantastic so high up in the air on the twelfth floor. It had three bedrooms but I converted them into two to make the bedrooms bigger and there was thick, heavy glass in the bathrooms, which was really stylish. Although I loved the spiral staircase I replaced it with a new one, all in chrome with two-inch-thick glass panelling around it. I had a new lighting system put in too; I also had an integrated Bang and Olufsen sound system installed in every room. When I'd finished with it, it was fit for a king.

The reason I fell for the place was that I wanted to lead a double life: during the week I'd be Joe Bloggs with my Range Rover and at weekends I'd be living in Docklands, eating in West End restaurants with my son Zak. Sometimes I just felt like jumping in the Porsche and stopping being a farmer's boy for the weekend and heading up to town. I didn't even come into town every weekend, only when I felt like it. I've no idea who my neighbours were or what they were like; I never saw them.

I didn't just limit my horizons to London and Kent,

though. I also went on what most people would call a 'holiday of a lifetime' when I took two weeks to go to South Africa *and* Australia.

I can't remember the exact cost, but it was at least £10,000. It would have been a lot more but for some reason, the female friend I travelled with and myself went economy – I suppose I just didn't think to go Club Class.

It was an overnight flight to South Africa, a few days there, then on from Johannesburg, stopping at Bangkok to refuel, to Australia and then the rest of the time there before flying back direct. Yes, there was a lot of travelling involved.

My son Zak had done a similar holiday spread over a longer period of time, so I had a rough idea of the programme. It was just an amazing adventure holiday, something I had always wanted to do.

As I've mentioned, I went with a friend, a lady called Anita. There was no hanky-panky involved, though – I didn't want to go on my own and I wanted someone to talk to. I treated her to the trip and I didn't want anything in return; I was just glad of the company. She had a boyfriend too, by the way; he knew all about it and he was there at the airport to meet us when we returned.

When we landed in South Africa the tour guide took us straight to Fish Hoek, which is a gorgeous coastal village about 20 miles from Cape Town and famous for its fishing, angling and beach. It was the mating season for whales at the time, so you could go and watch them too; it was wonderful.

Everybody has some ambitions they'd like to fulfil if they

win the Lottery, something they have always dreamt of doing in their lives. Mine was to ride a horse along a beach with the tide coming in. I achieved that dream in South Africa. Anita, who was a competent horsewoman, used to ride my daughter Tina's horse, so she knew what she was doing. Soon after we landed we went out in a 'hack', a group of us. And when we got to the beach, the woman who was leading the group asked, 'Are there any competent riders among you?' I could ride a bit, but I wouldn't call myself that good. A couple of people put their hands up, though, and I thought, 'Right, I'll have a go' and stuck my hand up too. Next thing, they were haring off along the beach and I started to follow them. I was galloping as though it was 90mph, but stopping the bloody animal was another thing altogether, although I managed it somehow. But it was a dream of mine that had at last come true.

We wanted to put everything into the holiday that we could as we were only away for two weeks, so while we were out in South Africa we decided to go white-water rafting.

The previous night Anita and I had a few drinks and we didn't get to bed until about 2am; we had to get up at 6am, so you can imagine how it felt on a boat with great big rapids thundering all around us. I thought we'd be on enormous solid, thick rubberised rafts with a lot of other people, but they were quite small with only room for a couple of people at a time. Some people were falling out of their rafts and had to be hauled back in, but somehow we managed to stay aboard our fragile craft as we went through a series of ginormous rapids.

While we were there we went on a safari, staying in a hut at night and out looking for game during the daytime, and we also spent time wine-tasting in the Stellenbosch wine-growing region. Talk about living life to the full! At one stage on the wine tour we were asked to select six wines to taste. I went in there full of confidence, as if I knew what I was talking about, even though I didn't. Instead of taking a little sip and then spitting it out, we gulped all six glasses down – that's practically a bottle – and we came out of there as pissed as farts.

We also went in a chopper ride over the Cape, although we couldn't go too low because it would upset the ostriches! We abseiled down Table Mountain near Cape Town too and saw the prison on Robben Island where Nelson Mandela was held for 27 years.

But there was another side to South Africa. One morning I'd run out of cigarettes so I went out of the hotel to get some. I got a right telling-off from the tour guide when I returned, though, because you're not allowed to go out on your own as it is too dangerous. I can understand why. I looked out one day and saw a beautiful villa in lovely surroundings, and then turned my head and in the distance saw a shanty town. There was a massive difference in the two worlds and yet they are so near each other.

Then it was on to Sydney, where we were to meet Zak and his boyfriend. Although Zak had a girlfriend at the time of my Lottery win, he is actually gay and he greeted me in Australia with a bouquet of flowers. He came up to me, put his arms around me and said, 'Here, these are for you!' I felt so embarrassed!

Down Under we stayed in a hotel that Zak had arranged for us. I've forgotten the name of the hotel but it was one of the best in Sydney. It was very nice, but it just wasn't our cup of tea. The main reason being that we were 20 storeys up and although it had beautiful views we just didn't like being that high. So we changed that for an apartment with two bedrooms, which was ideal; it was central and very nicely furnished. To relax we'd go out with Zak to a few gay bars and meet his friends.

As we only had about six days free in Australia in total – about the same as we spent in South Africa – we were determined to cram as much as possible into every moment. We did a helicopter tour of Sydney and the harbour, which was wonderful, and we also went on a 'tour', if that is the right word, where you walk over the top of Sydney Harbour Bridge. Before they allow you to go on it you have to have a test to make sure you've not been drinking alcohol and to see if you have a dodgy heart and then they give you a pair of overalls so you don't keep anything in your pockets that might fall out. They also give you a belt and to that you attach a kind of a dog's lead that you always have clipped to the bridge as you move along so that if you do fall it will stop you and it keeps you dangling and safe. That's the theory, anyway! You also have a leader or guide with you and the whole thing takes about two hours. I suppose lots of people wouldn't like to do something like that, but I thought it was marvellous.

We also went to the Sydney Opera House, which was amazing. I can't remember what production we saw, but I do remember that the acoustics were out of this world.

I liked the Aussies a lot. I remember coming off the ferry one day and it was raining and an office girl spontaneously let us share her umbrella. You wouldn't get a girl who works in the City doing that for strangers.

We got a sea-plane around the area and we also visited Bondi Beach. I know it's world famous, but to tell you the truth I didn't think it was that impressive – more like a glorified version of Southend beach, as far as I was concerned.

One night we were drinking a lot and discussing what we should do the next day. Zak came up with the idea of a parachute jump and, being quite drunk, I decided to go along with it. It was to be from 13,000 ft high, with video cameras strapped to your head to record the trip. Understandably, I was quite nervous. Nevertheless I wanted to go first, just to get it over with. At 10,000 ft the pilot asked, 'How do you feel?' I looked out and replied, 'All the people look like ants. I wish I wasn't here!' And then I started up with, 'If the parachute doesn't open, all my money should go to the children' and stuff like that. Of course, I did the jump and survived to tell the tale. One person who didn't join me for that, though, was Anita. I wonder why?

Then it was back to Blighty. Mary and Eileen were running their business next to my house and lots of people would drive up to their place to visit, but it didn't bother me. If I'd had a family living there it might have been different, but I didn't mind. It was nice to see people and they'd all go across to the pub at dinner-time perhaps and I'd go in there and enjoy the company. I had started going out with Mary and wanted to help her. In fact, looking back now, I think I was besotted with her then, even though she had a boyfriend at the time, but I was never actually in love with her. It's hard to explain and some people might not understand it, but that's the way it happened.

Not long afterwards, their interior design business started to slow down. Mary had a few problems financially and she had told me certain things about her private life so I felt I had to tell her more about my life. I told her I'd won the Lottery and had picked up £10 million, and I ended up giving her some money. I can't call it a gift or a loan because we never got as far as discussing on what basis I gave it to her. Whether I expected *all* the money back, or thought I might get *some* back, or didn't think I'd get *any* of it back, I couldn't really say. I gave her a cheque for £200,000. I guess in my heart of hearts I never expected to see it again. So far I haven't. Perhaps one day she might turn up and give me the money back, who knows? There were no lawyers involved, no contract or anything like that.

Eileen fell out with Mary over what was happening between the two of us. I went into the investment with the pair of them, but it didn't work out. So I asked them to leave the annexe. As you'd expect, I had an argument with Mary about that.

One thing I do know, though, with the benefit of our old friend hindsight, it was a mistake. Sad to say, this wasn't the only time I lost my heart, my head – and a fair chunk of what was in my wallet – to a woman.

Some time in 1999, my daughter Tina met a woman in her early fifties at the hairdressers she went to in Epping and invited her to a party she was holding at Tilegate Farm. Tina told me, 'She's a lovely lady' – acting as a matchmaker in a sort of way. I introduced myself and we had a couple of dances.

I asked her out for a meal and soon she was coming with me when I went to see Zak, who by this time was living in Fulham. He had a boyfriend there and we would all go out and have a good time at restaurants and other places; she got on really well with Zak.

Now, it might be hard for some people to understand, but there was no sexual relationship between us, not even kissing. I might have given her the odd peck on the cheek, but never a full-blown snog. We went on in this platonic way for some six months, then I spoke to her about buying her a ring. So one day we went to Hatton Garden, the street in London famous for its jewellers in general – and the quality of its diamonds in particular – to do just that. We started looking at rings for £15,000 to £20,000, but she didn't like the look of them. To cut a long story short, it ended with me buying her a diamond ring for £200,000!

She didn't like any of the stones she saw to begin with, so the guy in the shop said he had some special stones that he could set in the ring for me, although he implied that they would be somehow above my status. I realised later that this simply wasn't the sort of attitude jewellers normally have. Without being crude, it then turned into a 'big willy' contest. He told me how much it would cost before I bought it, but I said that wouldn't be a problem. I just wanted to show him, despite what he thought, that I did have the cash to buy a ring that price. Again, with the benefit of hindsight …

Then she stopped seeing me! I was a bit naive back then and said to her, 'Well, if you don't want to see me, give me the ring back.' Her response was that she wouldn't and if there was any trouble then she had some brothers who would 'sort me out'.

Call me a fool if you like, I still get embarrassed talking about it now. That was that. Some time later, though, I bumped into her and she said she had sold the ring for £80,000, but that she wanted to start our relationship again. My reply? A very big 'no!'

There were more romantic complications later that year, and it all started after I bought a computer. I didn't have much idea about how they worked or how to set them up, but there was a woman I knew who did. She did the books of a pub nearby and that was all on a computer. She was married with two children and we got on well – her husband even helped install it for me. (Because of her family, I will leave her name out of this.) Once the computer was in place, I was able to e-mail her, and so we began corresponding.

One day she came to the house and started coming on to me; although I'm not one to boost myself up, I realised she was besotted with me. I liked her too and so we started seeing each other. She was lovely really and I don't think it was anything to do with the money – she just liked me as I was. She would come to the house and we would make love. Eventually, I said, 'Why don't we get this together?', so she told her husband that she was in love with me – and he was absolutely gutted. He didn't come round and threaten to beat me up or anything like that. Nor did he come round and burst into tears. He was just really upset.

I told her brother about it and her mother knew as well. This all lasted for a couple of months and I even asked her to come on holiday with me. But then she opted to stay with her husband – I think it was for the sake of the kids – which meant we were finished. There was no money involved in our relationship; it wasn't a case of me handing over loads of cash this time. I didn't give her expensive gifts or buy her presents, but I was very fond of her.

I don't consider myself a fool, but I have to say there was a period of my life where the old saying 'a fool and his money are soon parted' was one that fitted me very well. We all do stupid things at times and at that time I was doing a *lot* of stupid things. I wanted female company, but I wanted somebody to love me for what I am; I was fed up with people taking the piss out of me. In short, I started to get very depressed and almost became a recluse again.

All I wanted was someone to love and someone who would

love me. I was fed up with being Mr Nice Guy all the time; I was tired of being shat upon. I was even fed up with being a Lottery winner! There were times when I wished I'd never won the poxy money. I was trying to 'buy' love, if you like, and that was a big mistake. It was a complete reversal from how I'd felt when I first won. Then I'd taken to the money, and what it could give me, like a duck to water.

All my kindnesses seemed to have been taken for granted, though, and I found myself thinking, 'If this is what money does to you, then you can keep it!' Things became so bad that I began to long for the days when I'd just been an 'Ordinary Joe'. I desperately wanted to be back where I was before I'd won the Lottery.

5

The Love Test

I used to go into Panini's café in Epping almost every day for my breakfast. I always had their 'Early Bird' special: egg, bacon and sausage with tea or coffee, all for £1.99. (I always had tea.) Very nice it was too, excellent value for money and there was always a good, lively atmosphere.

As soon as I saw the manageress there – and there is no other way of putting this – I fancied the socks off her. That woman was, of course, Lisa, who was destined to be my wife, the woman who would at last bring happiness to my life. But there was a long, long way to go before all that happened.

I felt at ease with her immediately; I could talk to her and discuss my problems with her. I showed her the letter I had received from the mother of two that I had my brief relationship with and as a woman I knew she would understand it, be able to relate to it. Somehow I felt I could confide in Lisa. There were things in that letter I don't want to go into – I'll just say they concerned the two of us. Lisa's verdict? 'What a load of rubbish.' Her view was, 'If she was a married woman she shouldn't have gone there in the first place.' Fair comment.

Although Epping was not far from where I lived, and some people there might know that I'd won the Lottery, it was far from common knowledge on the streets of the town how rich I was. Okay, a few people might have heard, but they didn't know the exact amount and it wasn't as though I'd been in the newspapers at the time and had become really high profile – a celebrity, of sorts – in the way that some Lottery winners do.

You have to remember that at this time I was totally depressed. I felt I was being taken for a ride and that people were taking the piss out of me. Yet with Lisa I felt none of that. When she found the time she would sit down and have a chat with me and I found myself thinking, 'How can I make a move towards this woman?' I was a little bit cheeky and would say things, as a joke of course, like, 'Any time this week, darling?' and 'Have you taken your happy pills this morning?' I don't think it worked at first, because I would sometimes hear her say, 'This man aggravates me!'

When I first saw Blackhall, I knew there and then it was the place for me. Well, it was the same with Lisa, but even more instant – and a lot more important. I knew she was the one. I found myself thinking, 'Why on earth didn't she come along before all this other shit happened?' It was love at first sight. As soon as I met her I knew that I loved her.

I decided I wasn't going to mess it up this time. I was still scarred, affected in some way by what had gone on before and by the dealings I'd had with other women. I wasn't going to make the mistakes that I'd made before.

And that's how it all started. I was about to begin the biggest lie of my life. I was determined that there'd be no question of it being my money or lifestyle that Lisa was interested in; it would have to be me and me alone.

I decided to become Joe 'Mr Ordinary' Johnson again: Joe 'The Loser', Joe 'Average Man-in-the-Street', call it what you like – I don't care, but you get the message. The one thing I didn't want to be was 'Loads-of-Money' Joe – the man with more cash than brains, the sort of guy who would be an easy target for the wrong sort of woman. It wasn't that I thought Lisa was like that – it was more a case of 'once-bitten, twice shy'. In my case, more than once-bitten … So I had to start an elaborate series of subterfuge, half-truths and downright lies to put her through the ultimate test.

To start with, I didn't want to be seen driving around in a flash car, the type that only millionaires can afford, so I didn't take the Porsche into Epping. Instead, I made the conscious decision to get behind the wheel of my black Range Rover Discovery, which was always covered in mud and dirt, which somehow made it look a lot less valuable than it was.

That was the question of the wheels settled. But then there was the problem of the house. Remember, I was living in Blackhall, the sort of home most people would give their right arm for; the type of house that appears in the glossy magazines or as a setting in a plush television drama. So I told

Lisa that I was looking after it for a friend, house-sitting as it were. That was that sorted.

But then how come I was able to come into her café as and when I liked? Surely I'd got a job? So again I decided to stretch the truth – all right, lie if you like. I said I worked at a printers and that they didn't want me in five days a week full time. They'd simply call me in whenever the work warranted it – which explained why I could come into Epping and the café at all times of the day. I also told her that I'd got a few investments that brought some money in. Well, at least that was true – although I certainly didn't tell her what the investments were, or the vast sums involved, or that it was all being handled personally for me by one of the country's most exclusive 'Top People' banks.

I didn't go to Epping at weekends, normally only during the week – Monday to Friday. And soon it got to the stage where I couldn't wait for the weekend to end so that I could go into the café again.

Pretty soon I was faced with a dilemma, 'How could I pluck up the courage to ask her out?' One day I summoned up the nerve to say to Lisa, 'Can I ask you a personal question?' She said, 'What?' and I replied: 'You have got a nice body, do you work out?' She laughed her head off. She thought it was funny then and she still does now. The only reason that I asked her that was at one stage I had worked out at a gym in Chelmsford and you notice there if people work out or not. I reckoned that with her good figure it stood a chance that she did.

Mind you, not being honest with her left plenty of situations open to misinterpretation. Once Lisa saw me out with my daughter Tina in Epping. She didn't know anything about Tina, saw me with a young woman and jumped to the obvious conclusion. What made it worse was that we had a baby with us! Lisa and I passed each other by and then I turned round to look at her at the same moment as she turned round to look at me – so there was something there even then. The baby was Tina's, of course, and pretty soon, when Lisa knew a little – but not a lot – more about me, she realised her mistake.

I'd been going into the café for some weeks by this time and I got into the habit of popping into the flower shop nearby. I'd buy a single rose for her, one day red, one day white, one day pink – I varied it all the time. I'd write on the small card that came from the florist, 'All My Love, Joe 90.' Then, as I arrived for my breakfast, I would hand it to her, desperately hoping she'd get the message. I know all that makes me sound like a nervous teenage boy plucking up the courage to ask out a girl from school, but it really was a question of what tactic I should use rather than me just being nervous.

Eventually, after having my breakfast one day and handing over the £1.99, I got round to asking her, 'Would you like to come out for dinner?' and her reply was, 'Yes.' Simple as that.

I had become used to going to all the top places in London. I'd go to Langan's Brasserie in Mayfair – where all the showbiz stars go – the restaurant at Harvey Nichols, Princess Diana's favourite place to dine, and I'd regularly go to the best places in Soho ... so now I'd got a problem: where the hell was I going to take Lisa that wouldn't reveal I was financially 'sound', to put it mildly?

At the time, Lisa was house-sitting in Epping for her sister who was away on holiday, so I arranged to pick her up from there. I actually found it difficult to choose somewhere after all the places that I'd got used to going to. Then I had an idea: it's nice to go out for a drive anyway and there's no better way of getting to talk to a woman than while you're driving along or stuck in traffic. I'd asked her if she liked Chinese food and she said she did, so I decided to take her to a Chinese restaurant I knew in Greenwich. That way we could have a meal together but I'd also have a fair bit of time to talk to Lisa during the drive.

But the Chinese place I chose that night wasn't an intimate one with individual tables or booths, let alone candles or anything of that nature. It won't figure in a Michelin Guide to fine eating; it was a place where everyone sat at long tables with giant, communal benches running alongside. You had to lift your leg over and slide in just to get seated.

Lisa got quite dressed up for her night out. 'Smart-casual' is the best way to describe it and her hair looked marvellous too. She looked the business, I can tell you, yet there she was sitting next to backpackers and tourists and everyone was listening in on everyone else's conversation. The menu wasn't in elegant holders with trendy designs, it was just chalked on boards on the wall. Hardly the intimate tête-à-tête that a first date should be.

I used chopsticks. I could just about manage them, not very well I must say, but Lisa didn't use them at all. All she wanted really was a spoon and fork, so she was a bit embarrassed about that. Once I got to know her better and we started to go to a few more Chinese restaurants together I'd use a knife and fork and a spoon too – it was easier. In fact, I never used chopsticks again.

The whole bill for the two us on that first date didn't even come to £20. At least I didn't ask her to go 'Dutch' and pay for her own food, even though the thought had crossed my mind!

Lisa felt uncomfortable because she had never been to a restaurant like that. But, of course, she didn't realise it was all part of my plan. All the time I had to be careful not to let the truth slip out. She asked me how long I had been at the printers and where exactly I lived. I told her about the house, again adding that I was looking after it for a friend. I also had to make sure I didn't mention the two Porsches and the new Range Rover that I had back at my house. I had to stick to my cover story no matter what and make sure a careless remark didn't slip out to give the truth away.

If I'd mentioned the exotic holidays I'd been on or some of the shops, like Cartier, that I'd visited, she'd probably have picked up on it straightaway and wondered how I could afford to move in circles like that. I didn't even dare wear anything that would signal I had money to spare. I just wore a Fred Perry polo shirt and an ordinary pair of jeans for that first date.

On the way home I asked her if she had enjoyed the

restaurant and she politely told me that she'd never been to one quite like that before. Oh dear. 'I've f**ked up, then!' I blurted out. I couldn't tell Lisa the real reason I'd chosen that restaurant, though. I dropped her off, gave her a little peck on the cheek and said something like, 'We must do this again.' Thank goodness, she said, 'Yes, all right.' I don't know what I would have done if she had said no. On my way home I kept saying to myself 'Yes! You've cracked it!'

After that I decided to move up the social ladder and for our next date we went for a pub lunch at The John Barleycorn pub in Epping; we followed that up with a few more meals at pubs for around £20 to £30 for the pair of us. There was a time when that might have meant a fair chunk out of my wage packet, but not any more. I'd been going to places like Langan's and automatically ordering champagne; whenever I went out with Lisa it was always white wine – house white wine, that is.

I wasn't telling lies as such when I was with her, but I had to guard against telling the whole truth. I tried to steer the conversation away from anything that would force me into a verbal corner and lead me to slipping about just how much money I was worth.

All the time this feeling was growing that this was the woman for me. It had been there from the start, to tell the truth, but it was getting stronger and stronger every moment I was with Lisa. I kept thinking, 'I've got to do this right' and prove to myself that she was the one.

I didn't set myself a timescale for this. It wasn't as though

I'd decided to, say, give it a month or six months before I told Lisa the truth. Footballers talk about 'taking every game as it comes'. Well, I was taking every precious moment as it came. The longer I could delay it, the better for me because it meant that I was getting to know her more with every day that came. And I was loving it.

So we started going out. And I guess I owe a lot of credit to Lisa's best friend Lysa Cameron for that. Lysa, who worked as a waitress at Panini's, said she noticed a magical spark between us from the very beginning, and her encouragement played a big role in the early stages of our relationship.

We weren't into the movies or things like that, so we'd normally end up going out for a meal. Sometimes on a Sunday Lisa and I would go to London, shopping. I guess it was window-shopping really though, because we didn't buy anything. After months of going into some of the most famous, and expensive, shops in the world, there I was walking around London just looking in the window at everything – and Lisa hated it! She was a buyer rather than a 'looker', really. She was on decent money from the café, about £400 a week, and she would spend most of that on clothes. I had to keep my hands in my pockets and resist the temptation to just breeze in, whip out the credit card and buy everything in sight.

One day I bought Lisa a small gift, a scarf to match the Aquascutum coat she was wearing. She opened the bag and half-smiled and said, 'Thank you, darling, I've borrowed this coat off my sister.' I thought, 'Oh no, I've f**ked up again!'

Later, we stopped at a little sandwich bar-cum-café and after eating I asked for the bill, which came to about £30. Lisa insisted that she paid and I agreed.

Once we were driving around and I asked her would she like to go for a fish meal at Smith's. Lisa thought I meant Smith's in Ongar, a classy restaurant famous for its seafood and one where the bill could quite easily mount up. She said, 'No, I'm not really dressed for Smith's,' as she had just finished work. I told her not to worry, I was talking about going to a fish and chip shop up the road from my home which was also called Smith's! We went there and both ended up having cod, chips, mushy peas and a gherkin. Lisa thought it was hilarious and wasn't at all disappointed.

One of the things I knew about her even then was that she wasn't looking for a rich man. Her husband, from whom she was estranged, was a market trader and they had a lovely son, Alfie, who lived with Lisa. So she wasn't interested in playing that 'footballer's wife' role. I knew it, but I just had to check – and check again – to reassure myself.

Looking back now, it was the most frustrating time of my life. I lost track of the number of times that I stood alongside her looking at the goods on sale in one shop or another and she'd say how much she liked something and I had to resist the urge to say, 'Let's go in and buy it, then!' I'd blown £400,000 on women who didn't deserve it; here was the woman who deserved to have that money spent on her and I couldn't do it! It was a complete reversal of what had gone before, yet I simply had to carry on in this way. All my life I had been looking for true love and I wasn't going to cock it up this time.

Don't get me wrong, there were plenty of good times too. Some of the happiest moments were in the winter of 2000 when Lisa would come over to Blackhall, before she actually moved in, and I would light the fire in the big fireplace. I'd throw some giant logs on it, they would crackle away and Lisa and I would snuggle up in front of it on the rug and make love. It was so romantic, some of the best memories in my life without a shadow of a doubt. Part of me did want to tell her the truth; another part kept holding myself back from revealing everything. I wasn't proud of what I was doing and I certainly didn't enjoy it, but I knew it had to be done.

We had both 'been round the block', if you like. We were more than happy just to go out to local pubs and have a quiet time together. We didn't want to go gallivanting around the place; we just wanted to be together all the time.

We met in the October of that year and about a month later I took her to Blackhall for the first time; I'm afraid there was one innocent victim of my subterfuge around this time. I used to have a cleaner, a nice Croatian lady in her fifties who was recommended to me by my daughter. Her name was Sophia, although I called her 'Soapy' for a bit of a laugh. She would come down five days a week and do four hours for me on every visit, for about £60. She would clean, do the ironing — pretty much anything I wanted around the house. If I liked a shirt a lot I would have it washed, dried and ironed in a day so I could wear it the next day. She would even ask if I wanted her to cook me anything. I think she looked upon me as a poor little man who needed looking after! Unfortunately, however, I had to get rid of her before I could entertain any thoughts of Lisa moving in because she would have wondered how I could afford a cleaner. So – regretfully – I let her go a week or two before Lisa arrived.

Once I made the decision that she couldn't be around at the same time as Lisa, I had to pick up the Hoover and do the cleaning myself. 'I don't want to do this!' I thought to myself. 'I've spent my life Hoovering and cleaning and now I'm back where I started!' But it was all part of my scheme; I had to stick to it.

I'd told Lisa about the house, about its oak beams and all the other marvellous features that gave it the character and charm I adored. It was a lovely house and she knew and appreciated that, but it was very much a 'man's house' at the time, very masculine in its feel and décor. Lisa liked to mix the old and the new and I must admit everything there was either genuinely old or felt old.

Fortunately, Lisa never asked me questions about the 'friend' whose house I was looking after. She didn't ask who he was, or where he was, or how long I would be there on my own. It was a good job, as I'd have had to lie or tap-dance my way out of that. In fact, Lisa didn't demand anything from me at all. I was doing all the running and playing all the games; she was with me simply because she wanted to be.

Christmas was approaching and Lisa wasn't going to be

with me on Christmas Day as she would be at her parents, but I wanted her to come over on Boxing Day. As I've already mentioned, there were two pubs near where I lived in Moreton and there was traditionally a tug of war between teams from the pubs. There was a bridge over a stream of running water and the two pub sides would line up near it, on the opposite banks of the little river.

The entire day's events lasted about five hours, with people running around the pub while carrying a pint of ale or bales of hay, that sort of thing. As it was such a long day I would have people back to my house for drinks and sandwiches. It didn't enter my mind at that stage that if someone who went to the pub had somehow heard about my Lottery win they might have told Lisa. If it had, I would have been a bag of nerves as the day wore on. I would have simply had to say to Lisa, 'Yes, it's true. I hold my hands up to it.'

It was on this Boxing Day that Lisa met my family for the first time. Obviously, I had to tell them in advance not to mention anything about my money to her. They agreed to it and they could see the reasoning behind it, but they didn't like doing it. Tina had seen in the past how hurt I'd been and she always kept an eye on me. I'd told her about Lisa, told her I loved Lisa to bits, but when I introduced her to Lisa I could almost sense her thoughts – 'You're not here to hurt my dad, are you?' Of course, she didn't say anything to that effect – she's not like that. She was just being protective, and you can't blame her for that. My son Nick was a lot more laidback about the whole thing, and simply let me get on with it.

That Boxing Day was a huge success – I'd been out to Marks & Spencer a few days before and got stuff to bung in the oven for people to eat: sausage rolls and other similar nibbles. We had a big, magic fire going all day and everyone had a great time.

I guess some people might expect me to heave a big sigh of relief as Nick, Tina and their families went out the door, to thank my lucky stars that they hadn't told Lisa about the Lottery, but my main concern was over what they thought of Lisa. What did they make of the woman who I knew was going to be my other half?

When I asked Tina what she thought Lisa soon afterwards, she said – very honestly – 'She is nice, but I don't know her, Dad.' And she would always tell me, bearing in mind what had happened to me before, 'Be careful.' That said, she would make a point in the future whenever Lisa was mentioned of telling me, 'She always looks nice' or, 'She is always well presented.'

So, I'd got away with it over the Christmas holidays, but there were trickier times ahead. There is one significant trait of mine that I haven't mentioned yet; one that had a major bearing on this whole period. Here I was keeping the truth away from Lisa by means of a massive deception – but truth be told, normally, I can't keep a secret to save my life! I am the world's worst at anything like that. I have the kind of urge to pass on information that normally only exists in gossip pages. If someone says to me they have a surprise for me, I have to know what it is immediately.

Somehow or other I'd managed to get through the earliest stage of our relationship without letting the cat out of the bag. But little did I know how easy these first few wonderful weeks had been – there were much harder times to come before I could reveal my huge secret.

6

The Holiday from Hell

I was regularly driving the Range Rover Discovery by now and would pick Lisa up in it, so she knew all about that vehicle. What she didn't know was what else was in the large garage at home. Inside were those two Porsches, a dead giveaway to my wealth if she should ever see them. It wouldn't have been easy to explain them away! Even I would have been hard-pressed to come up with a believable story, as they had the registration plates '17 JJ' and '16 JJ' – personalised 'Joe Johnson' specials, showing they belonged to me. I don't think Lisa would have fallen for some cock-and-bull story about 'JJ' also being the initials of the man whose house I was looking after.

Fortunately, they were locked out of sight behind three 'up-and-over' garage doors, but I realised that I would have to move them at some stage and began wondering where to put them so that Lisa wouldn't catch me in the act. I would either have to do it when I was sure she wouldn't turn up, probably when she was at work, or in the dead of night. Neither plan appealed to me too much.

But I still had to use the cars at some time, I couldn't leave my 'babies' alone. I couldn't resist the temptation they offered me. So I'd wait until Lisa went to work and then I'd go out for a drive in the country. Of course, I couldn't go to Epping in case she saw me, or a friend of hers spotted me driving round in a flash motor – so I'd go to somewhere like Chelmsford instead.

I loved taking them out for a spin, but I had to make sure that I got back in time before Lisa came home from work – the Cinderella Syndrome, as it were. I also had to make sure her son Alfie was at school so he didn't see me behind the wheel of a Porsche.

Thankfully, one problem disappeared – the possibility that Lisa might accidentally discover what was in the garage when she was having a look around – when she let slip that she was scared of spiders. I immediately came up with a false warning for her and said straightaway: 'Don't go near the garage then, darling, the place is crawling with them!' That was one hazard sorted out – for the time being, at least.

I always intended to tell her about my money, it was just a question of when. They say that love is blind and I guess it must be true, for I only had eyes for Lisa by then; I knew she was the one for me. So much so that I decided to buy her a ring. I gave her a diamond ring as a Christmas present that first year, but it was a real change from the rings and jewellery I'd bought over the previous 18 months. This time I didn't go to a world-famous store like Cartier or Harrods; I chose a jeweller in Epping High Street. And although it had a diamond in there somewhere, you'd have a pretty hard job to find it without a microscope. The cost? Somewhere in the region of £150 – if it cost more than that, it wasn't a lot more. Lisa still thought it was sweet, though.

Like me, Lisa was the youngest of a fairly large family as she had three sisters and two brothers. Like me too, she's paid her dues in life. If anyone is silly or petty enough to resent the good things and the happy times we've enjoyed in recent years, they should bear that in mind before jumping to conclusions.

She was born in Romford, lived there until she was 14, and in her youth worked on a hot-dog stall, in the markets and did some fly-pitching – that's working on unofficial markets. Her father was a landscape gardener and that meant that in the winter there wasn't as much work around as there was in the summer. For six months when she was 17 she worked in a clothing factory and then became a hairdresser. She loved it and did that for a year and a half in a unisex salon in Chadwell Heath, although she was only picking up £25 a week compared to the £100 she could get from the fly-pitching. She also worked for a spell in a luggage store called Beau Baggage before starting to work for her sister Josie in Epping and having the good fortune – that's how I think of it, anyway – to meet me.

Can you imagine the frustration I was feeling? I loved her so much that I wanted to shower her with presents; I wanted to get her a wonderful gift every day that we were together, yet I couldn't. Although I was wonderfully happy being with her, it was also, at the same time, one of the worse periods I'd ever been through because of this lie of a life I was leading.

In a way it was like depriving someone of food. It was as though I was saying, 'You will have to stick with Spam and chips', when I could be giving them the finest fillet steak every day instead.

The irony was that while I was buying her cut-price gifts, she bought me some really nice presents that year: a £500 jacket from Geoff's, an exclusive menswear shop in Epping High Street. Apart from the solitary roses that I used to bring her in the café and the small diamond ring, I didn't buy her any presents at all that year. I was getting so used to playing this part, this role I had created for myself, that I was actually becoming meaner and meaner. Well, at least I was saving a bit of money …

Before I asked Lisa to move in with me I wanted to get to know her son Alfie. It was very important to me – after all, I was in love with his mother. I first met him in Panini's, briefly saying 'hello', and I noticed what a polite boy he was. The second time I met him, my impression of him was how smartly dressed and good-looking he was with beautiful big blue eyes. He was well-mannered too, and I got on well with him. We talked about football, even though I didn't know much about it then; I asked him who he supported and he said Chelsea and I told him I was a Tottenham fan, which made him laugh. After meeting him a few times, I knew we would get on well together – a very big hurdle for me and I had overcome it.

During the time when I was first getting to know Lisa I went around to her apartment in Clayhall in Essex. Although she was separated she was still married at the time and I guess I wanted to scrutinise the place to see if there were any signs of a man living there. Call me suspicious if you like, but I was so wary of women at this period in my life that I somehow couldn't take anything at face value. I needn't have worried. It was a typical female apartment with a little boy's room too, as Alfie would have been about five at that time.

Then came the big decision – soon after Christmas I asked Lisa to move in with me. It would make my 'dual life' even more difficult, as I'd have to be careful what I said to people on the phone, and if someone turned up who knew about my win I would have to keep them away from Lisa, but I knew it was what I wanted.

Straightaway Lisa asked the obvious question: 'This friend of yours, how long is he going to be away and what will happen to us when he comes back?' That was tricky. So I told her he was in America and it would be a long time before he returned. When he did, well, we'd just have to pool our resources and find somewhere to stay. She then had to make the difficult decision of whether or not to give up the home she was renting nearby and have this uncertainty ahead of her. I know it sounds strange, but these mundane – and sensible – problems just didn't matter. We were so much in love and we wanted to be together; that's all that counted.

It was just wonderful having her be with me, having her under the same roof. The simplest things brought me the greatest happiness. That's what it's like when you're in love, after all. She'd be cooking in the large kitchen we had in the house and I'd ask her what we would be having for dinner. She would be getting together something like mash potatoes and fresh greens all with a lovely, thick gravy to go with them, and alongside would be some minted lamb chops. I was used to eating pub food and when I was on my own I'd never bother to get a proper meal. I adored those dinners – particularly her fabulous lamb chops – because Lisa was the one getting it ready for me.

All the time, however, I was worried that she'd find out how rich I was. It was preying on my mind constantly, because if she did somehow stumble on my secret there was no way of predicting her reaction. She might have said, 'If you don't trust me enough to tell me the truth about something as important as that, then how can I trust you over anything?' It would have been an entirely understandable reaction. That would have meant my whole plan would have backfired; instead of bringing us closer the secret would have driven us apart.

Later she was to say that she would have been annoyed if she had found out from someone else rather than me telling her; in her own words, she would have been 'fuming'. So who could say how our lives would have turned out then?

I wanted to tell her every day. It would flash in my mind, 'Shall I tell her today? Shall I tell her tomorrow?' There was no set plan, no timescale. I hadn't got a diary with one day ringed in red as the 'Big Day'. It could have gone on like that for ages. In theory, it could have been a year, but in all honesty I don't think I could have hacked it that long.

By the end of January Lisa had been living with me for a little while, and I was 100 per cent certain that she was the one for me. So I asked her to marry me.

Little Alfie had gone to bed, we'd had a bottle of wine and I was sitting on my Ronnie Corbett chair. Lisa was sat on the sofa and suddenly I just came out with it: 'Lisa, will you marry me?'

Then, abruptly, she replied, 'No, it's too early.'

I was not a happy bunny. I was very disappointed. But coming back to earth I realised that she was right; it was too early in our relationship to make a big decision like that. I wasn't tempted to make her change her mind by saying anything like, 'If it's the money side of things that you're worried about, there's something I've got to tell you …' I just accepted it. It did make me feel quite insecure, though. I even thought to myself, 'Well, I'm not going to ask her again!'

Then we started to have our differences, perhaps you might call them little arguments, about some things. I am not vicious or aggressive with children – I'm not in favour of smacking or anything like that – but I think that I'm a good parent and believe that children need a bit of discipline. Little Alfie was, and is, a fantastic kid and I love him to bits, but once he was out of order over something – I can't even remember what it was – and I told him off. Lisa told me not to do that again. I thought to myself, 'We are living together, why can't I?' But Lisa told me straight, 'No, I will do that.'

It made me think: 'Alfie and Lisa – where do I come in this?' There was no doubt – and I hate this phrase, but I guess it sums up the relationship between the two of them – they came as a 'package deal', so to speak. It's a horrible phrase, but it gets the message across. Most of our arguments, disagreements, call them what you like, were probably over Alfie. That's not to say that he was to blame, it's just the way it happened.

It was so frustrating because, for example, if he did something wrong in the garden I'd have to say to Lisa, 'Tell Alfie not to do that', and then she'd tell him. It just didn't seem normal to me. I couldn't say to him directly the sort of remarks that you make all the time to youngsters when they are your own, like, 'be careful with that' or, 'put that down' or, 'don't do that'. Instead, I'd have to go through Lisa. And if Alfie repeated whatever it was he'd done – and, of course, children do that all the time – I'd have to mention it to Lisa again. All this meant a bit of tension crept into our relationship.

I did push the boat out once for them, though: I took Lisa and Alfie on a day trip to France! We all got in the Range Rover, drove to the coast and got the ferry over for a day. It wasn't as though we were going over there to stock up on champagne or to dine at some wonderful restaurant. Our meal was sandwiches on board.

On another occasion, at the end of January, a large group of us went to Wings Chinese restaurant in Epping for a family meal to celebrate my birthday. It was a favourite place of Lisa and myself and we'd often go there just as a couple. This time, though, there were six adults and six children in the group as it was a birthday outing and the bill came to over £300. Nick and Tina said they would cover things, as it was my birthday, but Lisa was determined to show she was more than prepared to pay her own way; it was going to be her treat. She excused herself as if to go to the washroom and while she was away from the table paid the bill for the lot of us. That's the kind of woman she is. So when Nick and Tina asked the waitress for the bill, they were told it was all taken care of. I bit my lip when I heard that; I was itching to reach in my back pocket, get some money out and pay the lot.

This wasn't the only time that kind of thing happened. Lisa would often pay the bill when the two of us went out. Sometimes I'd do it, sure, but on other occasions she took care of things. They were what you'd call 'ordinary' meals, admittedly, nothing grand; we'd just go for a Chinese or an Indian, so it was nothing that was going to break the bank. She also helped out with the household bills and would often do the shopping for food, drink and all the other bits and bobs you need to run a house.

By this time, I was starting to get itchy feet; I wanted to go away with Lisa on a romantic holiday. I thought it would be great if it was just the two of us. Alfie wanted to go to Lisa's mum and dad at their caravan in Clacton and I thought this would be a great opportunity for us to have a break. I asked Lisa if she wanted to come with me and she said she did, so off I went to the local travel agent.

Now, remember that in the previous 18 months I'd been to America, South Africa and Australia, but all those places were ruled out by the life I was leading. I could easily have booked a boutique hotel anywhere in the world, or a stylish villa alongside those of Hugh Grant or some other film star. Instead, I decided to go to Tenerife as I'd spent some time there when I was young and had fond memories of the place.

I ended up booking a package holiday for a week, staying in a hotel in the Las Americas area of Tenerife. I don't even remember how much it cost, but it was nowhere near £300, it was so cut-price. We flew out from Gatwick and the kids took us to the airport for our flight. We didn't realise it, but we were about to embark on the original holiday from hell.

As soon as we got there we realised that we were in an ''Ere we go, 'ere we go!' crowd, the type who'd wear hats with, 'We done it in Corfu' on them. As the coach that picked us up made its way around the island, it kept stopping at different hotels to let the holidaymakers off so they could check in. Some of those hotels were so bad they were like kennels that you wouldn't even leave your dog in for the weekend. It wasn't looking good.

I could see Lisa looking at me as the coach kept arriving at these places, every one somehow or other worse than the one before. I turned to her and said, 'Don't worry darling, it will be all right …'

Of course, our hotel turned out to be the final one on the route, so we were the last people to get off the coach. It was a small hotel and when we walked in there were just two small children – neither of whom could speak English – on reception. We indicated that we wanted to go to our room and eventually someone came to show us to it. Things were going downhill pretty quickly and I feared the worst when the man showing us to the room had to unlock the gates right in front of our bedroom door. Nothing unusual in that normally, but these were padlocked and you don't normally associate padlocks with sunshine holidays!

Inside there was some cheap wooden furniture that had all been painted a hideous dark bottle-green, and there was a shelf made from chipboard on the wall. All along it were cigarette burns where fags had been left and had burnt down to the butt. Obviously the type of person who stayed there couldn't be bothered with anything so fiddly as an ashtray.

There were two single beds and one of them had a mattress that was so aged you could actually see that it was bowed in the middle from all the people who had lain on it over the years. It was old as the hills.

This was one of those moments when I felt a real compulsion to reveal everything to Lisa and tell her, 'Come on darling, we're off! Let's find a good hotel, I can afford it.' I felt I could hack it, I could stomach it, just about, as it was part of my project, my mission in life. I didn't think I could stand it for Lisa, though – I didn't want her to have to stay somewhere like this. But we decided to stick it out.

We went back down to reception and asked if there was a safe we could use. We didn't have much jewellery on us, but we had our passports and a couple of nice coats that we'd worn for the journey and we wanted somewhere secure to leave them. But we were told no, there wasn't; instead, we were handed a large key ring with a bunch of keys on it and were told that they opened the gate and the bedroom door and we were to keep them with us. That's the last thing you want after going out for a meal, to come back and start fiddling with a bunch of keys in the darkness, but we had no choice. It was getting late, so we just went out for a meal and came back and had a terrible night's sleep in this awful bedroom. Next morning, in the daylight, it was even worse. We went to look at the pool and it was so greasy and dirty, it looked like a vast tub of liquid Brylcream.

If the hotel and its facilities were bad, the other guests seemed to complement them very well. Lisa and I like to get dressed up if we go out. Not too much, not over the top, but it felt as though we were Posh and Becks compared with some of the people there. One man wore the same red shorts all week – day and night, all the time. Even in the room they called 'The Clubhouse', where they had the karaoke, he'd be there wearing those red shorts. He probably wore them on the flight back home.

There was one bar in the hotel that served food. I call it 'food', but it was just dried-up pizzas and sandwiches that were curling up at the ends. We had breakfast included in the price of the holiday but we didn't even eat that; we went out in the morning as quickly as we could. Any café would do, we simply couldn't face the thought of tackling whatever they might send out from the kitchens. We didn't eat a thing there all week. The only thing we consumed was a drink of Baileys at night before we went to bed.

It was so bad that Lisa and I would go out for the day to a different part of the island rather than stay around the hotel. We'd walk to Los Cristianos, which was much smarter and more our cup of tea. We'd get talking to people from London and the rest of England in the bars or restaurants and the conversation would always include the question, 'And where are you staying?' Someone would mention the rather posh hotel they were at and when they asked us we'd mumble something in reply. If they wanted to know exactly where it was, we'd say something like, 'Oh, it's a bit of a walk up the hill.'

We always liked to end the evening with a Baileys nightcap when we got back to a hotel, so when we returned to this awful place we were in we'd have to go in the room where the karaoke was on to get a drink, as that's where the bar was. There was a guy from up North who was always on the karaoke or behind the microphone. At the start of the week they try and find out everyone's name, so we said 'Lisa and Joe', and that meant that every night when we got back and walked into the room – the karaoke would go on until 3am – he'd call out our names. He was nine bob short of a shilling, this guy, and he'd call out in his broad Northern accent, 'Oh look, here comes Lisa and Joe; via London, via Essex.' Then he'd announce, 'Lisa's going to get up and sing one of Celine Dion's numbers.' You had to laugh – otherwise you'd have cried.

You know when you have had a good night out on holiday and eventually you get tired, you really look forward to going back to your room and crashing out? Well, we just couldn't bear the thought of going to our room, it was so horrible. Lisa never unpacked her suitcase all week; she was so worried that someone might come in the room and steal her clothes. She'd never stayed anywhere like it in her life; it even had cockroaches.

It was so bad we couldn't even think about romance in a room like that. On two occasions we went down to the beach in the dead of night to make love – it was cleaner than the hotel.

At least the weather was nice. On one occasion Lisa went in her bikini and sarong to sunbathe for a bit by the pool. She even somehow plucked up the courage to put her feet in the water, but as soon as they were submerged she couldn't see them any more, the pool was so dirty.

I did ask her if she wanted to move, but we were spending as much time as possible away from the hotel anyway and it would have meant finding somewhere else, so we decided to stick it out. That, and the that fact the coach was due to pick us up from there, meant we stayed put. I admired her that, for having the strength to stay on and not throw a fit about it all.

Two weeks after we got home we switched on the *Holidays From Hell* programme on television, which chronicles terrible places and experiences people have had when they go away, and, surprise, surprise, there was our hotel!

7

White Lies about The White Hart

One of the challenges of living at Blackhall with Lisa was keeping her away from the two pubs near where I lived. She could never understand why we had to cook a Sunday lunch every week when there were a couple of excellent boozers within walking distance. I avoided them like the plague, even on a cold winter's evening when they looked so inviting with their lights on and you could hear the cheering sound of laughter and glasses being chinked; it puzzled her no end.

The truth of the matter was that there was a strong chance that some of the staff in the pubs, and a few of the customers, knew a little bit too much about me. They didn't have all the full details, but they knew enough to let something slip about the money they thought I had – the fact that I was worth a bob or two. Just one careless remark would reveal to Lisa I wasn't all I was pretending to be. It would be like lighting the blue touchpaper and waiting for the rocket to go off.

Neither of us is a heavy drinker, although we like a nice glass of wine or good champagne when the occasion merits it, but there is something so wonderfully English about popping down to the local for a drink and something to eat. It was ironic, to say the least, that the situation I'd created meant that our two nearest pubs were, in effect, out of bounds.

No other country in the world seems to have mastered the art of drinking at a village pub the way we British have. I always used to enjoy my visits to the local Blackhall boozers when I was 'single and rich' and could just pop over there whenever I wanted for a lager and something to eat. It saved me preparing food and meant I didn't have to do the washing-up afterwards. So I had all sorts there – everything from a late breakfast to an evening meal. Once Lisa moved in, I couldn't be classified as 'single' anymore and that meant I couldn't use the pub as my 'kitchen' anymore either.

We would often go for a drive to country pubs, so she knew I liked pubs and didn't object to going into them on principle or anything like that. I was creating a trap for myself and one day, a few weeks after she had moved in, matters came to a head.

One particular weekend we hadn't had time to shop properly for food, so there wasn't much in the kitchen to get lunch underway with. The days when I would simply open a can of baked beans or have some cold sardines out of a tin were far behind me, as I couldn't expect Lisa and Alfie to eat like that, but this Sunday, with the cupboards bare, problems loomed.

'Let's go to the pub for once and have a bite to eat there,' Lisa suggested.

'They're not very keen on kids,' I lied, 'they probably won't let Alfie in. We'll have to sit outside.' It was winter and I thought that would put her off.

'But it's a beautiful day,' she countered, looking out at the sun streaming through the windows and onto The White Hart across the way.

'They say it's going to cloud over,' I ad-libbed, 'and with our luck it'll turn nasty just as our meal arrives.' I warmed to my subject – in fact, you may say I got a bit carried away – adding, 'and rain is forecast, so we could get wet too.'

'Don't talk nonsense,' she replied, 'it's not going to rain. We can go inside anyway.'

'No we can't; don't forget Alfie,' I replied.

'Would I forget Alfie?' she said. 'He doesn't want to come with us, so there's no problem there.'

I was running out of excuses fast. 'To tell the truth,' I said, 'the food isn't up to much.' This was the biggest lie of all. They do lovely meals with a great à la carte menu, organic food and supplies of fresh meat, fish and vegetables from Smithfield, Billingsgate and Covent Garden markets daily. Still, in for a penny in for a pound. If I was Pinocchio, my nose would have been getting bigger with every word that passed my lips. On I went, 'Yeah, it's nothing to write home about. The last time I went in I had the runs for twenty-four hours afterwards. Something didn't agree with me. It always puts me off a place if you get tummy trouble afterwards, don't you think? I think it was their prawns, probably not fresh.' Then, for good measure, I added, 'It's a bit of a dump too.'

I was slandering an excellent local something rotten, but I was cornered. The White Hart is a beautiful white-walled 16th-century pub that could feature on the cover of a tourist board brochure any day of the week. I still nipped in on occasions during the day when Lisa was at work, but I'd decided to declare it a no-go area at night for us as a couple. 'If you really want to go to a pub, let's go for a drive first and we'll find one.'

'When did you last eat there?' Lisa asked. I fell for that because I left myself open when I replied, 'Ages ago', so she immediately came back, 'Then let's see if it has improved. You've got to give these places a try. It could be wonderful by now, for all you know. Dodgy prawns, what are you going on about?'

I had to come out with my final strategy to avoid crossing the road and entering the pub, which could easily have customers propping up the bar or in the dining area who knew of my wealth and possibly my Lotto win. They would certainly have known I wasn't looking after the house for a friend; there were several people I knew for sure would instantly recognise me as the owner.

I improvised. 'The honest truth, Lisa, is … I don't like it because …' Lisa stopped and looked at me then waited for me to finish the sentence. I'd realised by now I had reached and gone past the point of no return, so I thought I'd better come out with the biggest lie I could. 'The truth is …' I stammered, 'that the landlord is …'

'Is what?' she asked. And by now she was getting a bit tetchy, probably because she was hungry.

'Well, he's a bit of a … you know …' I really was rambling by now, and giving Lisa the impression that there was something I didn't like about the man. Nothing could be further from the truth. He was as lovely a guy as you could ever wish to meet, but I was reckoning by this stage I might as well get hung for a sheep as a lamb.

'What are you talking about?' she persisted.

'We had a big row and I vowed never to go in there again,' I blurted out. 'I don't really want to go into detail, but there was a big bust-up between him and me in front of everyone in the place. It was very embarrassing.'

'You mean you're barred?' asked Lisa. This was getting out of hand by now and even I had to rein things in a bit then.

'No, not barred,' I stuttered, 'it's just that there's an atmosphere between the two of us. You could cut it with a knife.'

Lisa seemed to accept this and carried on being busy in the kitchen. This lulled me into a false sense of security, because a couple of minutes later she asked, 'What was it about then?'

'What was *what* about, darling?' I replied. I genuinely didn't know what she was talking about for a moment or two.

'What do you *think* I mean?' she continued. 'I'm talking about the row you had with the landlord. What was it all about?'

'You know, I can't even remember now,' I said, now simply hoping to get out of this alive. I was mistaken.

'If you can't remember what it was about, why don't we go across the road and pretend nothing ever happened?' Lisa suggested. 'He's a landlord, he'll want customers for the pub and as long as it was nothing outrageous you said to him I'm sure he'll be fine. There'll be no problems.'

'No, I just wouldn't enjoy my meal,' I said. 'I'd be thinking about it all the time we were sat down. I don't think I'd be able to eat anything.'

Lisa looked at me as if to say, 'What sort of man is this?' and muttered something along the lines of, 'I've never heard anything so stupid in my life', but then – to my immense relief – she threw in the towel over the great White Hart debate.

Phew, that was close. It hadn't solved the problem of what to eat, though. And then I heard her call out to me across the kitchen, 'We'll go to The Nag's Head, then.'

Now, The Nag's Head was the other pub in the village, just a few hundred yards away – again, 16th-century, half-timbered and very nice. The same danger lurked by the beer pumps, though: one of the clientèle or a member of the bar staff might mention my wealth and then I'd be in the soup.

'No, I don't want to go there either,' I told her.

'*What!*' said Lisa. 'What's wrong with The Nag's Head?'

'It's too far,' was all I could think of.

'But it's just down the road!' she cried, exasperated. 'We could walk it in less than a minute!'

'No, it's too much effort,' I countered, feebly.

'A minute ago you were saying you wanted to get into the car and go for a drive and find a country pub and that was all right, yet walking down the road is too much bother for you. What's going on?' Lisa asked. 'By the time you get into the car and start it, I could have walked to The Nag's Head!'

'There's another reason I can't go there,' I protested. 'The landlord doesn't like me.'

'Not again!' said Lisa. 'Don't tell me you've had a row with him over something you can't remember as well?' She'd got me there. Irrefutable logic had trapped me in a corner.

All I could think to reply to that was, 'It's just that I used to drink in The White Hart all the time until I had the row and the landlord of The Nag's Head doesn't like me as I drank at a rival pub.' Again, nothing could be further from the truth, of course – that landlord was a charming man too – but desperate men do desperate things.

Lisa looked at me as if I'd taken leave of my senses. There was a kind of logic in everything I was saying, but it wouldn't need much cross-examination to tear it apart.

'Look,' I said, 'I'll get the car started and we'll go for a drive to find somewhere nice for a lovely Sunday roast.' As we drove out of the village we could see cars beginning to pull up outside The White Hart and The Nag's Head and families piling out to head for their meals. Lisa looked at me but, thankfully, said nothing. I'd got away with it – for the time being, at least.

There was no way that this particular lie on my part could last forever without problems cropping up, though. Just a week or so later the debate was reopened.

We came out of Blackhall in the car and Jim, the landlord of The White Hart, was pottering around outside. He spotted me and gave me a big smile and friendly wave. We pulled away and Lisa said, 'Isn't that the landlord?' and I had to admit that it was. I couldn't pretend it was a passing stranger or something stupid like that.

'I thought you said he didn't like you?' she said.

'Yes that's right,' I told her. I could already sense what was coming.

'Well, he seemed to be pretty friendly just then,' she observed. I was running out of excuses, so I muttered that perhaps he was simply in a good mood that morning and, as usual, tried to change the subject.

Matters were coming to a head for sure, and early one evening a few days later Lisa turned to me in the kitchen and said, 'Let's go to The White Hart for a meal. It's just across the road and I can't be bothered to cook tonight.'

I couldn't bear to go through the lie about my falling-out with Jim again so the best excuse I could come up with was, 'It's very popular, you won't get in without booking.' This wasn't the most inspired excuse even by my desperate standards, as if it was fully booked it would only take a couple of minutes to walk across there and find that out. I was tempted for a second to telephone and have a phony conversation with the pub and pretend they were choc-a-block, but I realised that would be a wrong move as I could easily be caught out – Lisa would only have to look through the pub windows and see if there was room or not.

I gave in, and half an hour later we walked out of the front door. I felt like a condemned man taking that last walk to the gallows; there was no saving me now. We crossed the road and walked through the pub's front door; my heart was thumping away and I feared the worst. Normally we're happy to stand at the bar before sitting down to eat in a pub, but this time I spotted an empty table in the corner and immediately ushered Lisa towards it. I didn't want her striking up a conversation with anyone who might land me in it. I told her, 'You sit there, darling, while I get the drinks in.' So there she was, all alone in the corner, while I made my way to the bar. Remember, this was the pub where I said I was practically a hated figure, so the reaction I got didn't fit in with that description one little bit: a cheery greeting and big smiles all round. Oops!

I looked over my shoulder at Lisa, who would obviously have preferred to be mingling at the bar with me. She was looking at me and clearly taking in the fact that I was receiving a traditional friendly welcome. I ordered our drinks, praying they would come in seconds so I could avoid getting into any conversations that might land me in trouble.

As I waited for the glasses of wine I'd ordered, I'd hear, 'Hello, stranger' and, 'Where've you been hiding at nights?' from regulars who I'd have been only too happy to talk to a few months before. 'Oh, I've been up to my neck,' I said softly as I grabbed my drinks, avoided getting into any sort of conversation and headed back at top speed to Lisa.

'They seem very nice in here,' she said. This was getting

worse by the minute and I just kept my fingers crossed that things didn't get worse.

'Yes, they do,' I admitted, sheepishly.

'We'll have to start coming more often,' she said. I said nothing. By this stage I reckoned it was best to keep my mouth shut and let events take their own course. What would have helped was for the meal to be terrible – that would have given me an excuse to say we shouldn't come to The White Hart again. I was out of luck on that count, as I knew I would be. The food was marvellous, the service faultless; it looked as though we'd be coming to The White Hart a lot more in the future.

I had a lot of thinking to do as we ate. Now that Plan A – the scenario of an unfriendly pub with food that left a lot to be desired – lay in ruins, I'd have to put Plan B into operation. The only problem was, I didn't have a Plan B.

As we finished our meal, Lisa said, 'There, that wasn't too bad, was it? In fact, I thought it was great.'

'Er, yes, it's improved,' I replied, as I hurriedly paid the bill and tried to get out before anyone mentioned the dreaded 'L' word – lottery.

That night Lisa said to me, 'we'll go there more often in future', and I knew I had to snip that plan in the bud. So I tried out the Plan B I'd been working on since we'd got home.

'The difficulty is that you know what country communities are, word will get out that I'm "hitting the bottle" and if that gets back to the bloke I'm looking after this house for, he won't be happy,' I said.

Lisa gave me one of those looks of hers and said, 'What, just for eating a meal and having a glass or two of wine?'

'Yeah, crazy isn't it?' I said, in a resigned sort of way. 'That's why it's a good idea if we spread our wings a bit. Goodnight, darling!' And I quickly switched the lights out. I thought I'd managed to get over the problem of how to avoid my local pubs quite well, but, as I said, I did still pop in during the day for a quick drink and a bite to eat. I wasn't worried about that, though, as I knew Lisa was at work in Epping, so there would be no problems there. At least, that's what I thought.

8
Near Misses

Although Lisa met Nick and Tina a few times, I didn't want them to get involved in long conversations with her too early in our relationship, for obvious reasons: she might learn more than I wanted her to and it would be unfair on my children to ask them to keep such a secret. I simply said that they lived in North Weald and left it at that; I certainly didn't let on that they had homes to die for.

As I've already mentioned, one of our favourite places to eat was the John Barleycorn pub, not far from where we were living. The problem was that from our home at Blackhall the route to the pub meant you had to go right past the gates of Tollgate Farm, where Nick and Tina were living. I used to look at it as we hurried past and catch a glimpse through the bars of the electronic gate. I couldn't resist the temptation to comment and I'd say something like, 'Oh look at that, that's a nice property, isn't it?' Then I'd have a sneaky little laugh to myself, making sure that Lisa didn't pick up on anything I said or did. I guess I'm a bit of a wind-up merchant at times. I know it's going to backfire on me one day, but I've managed to get away with it so far. I had to play the game all that time, though. I really had to stay away from Nick and Tina's places as it might give everything away if I went there and Lisa found out about it.

I've mentioned that I felt secure popping to the pub when Lisa was at work, so one lunchtime when I couldn't be bothered to cook I headed for The White Hart. Normally I would have walked, but I wanted to go into Epping after I'd eaten so I got the Discovery out, parked outside the pub and went in and ordered a bite to eat. A few minutes later the food arrived and with my lager in front of me I picked up my knife and fork and hungrily started to tuck in. My appetite abruptly vanished, though, when out of the corner of my eye I saw Lisa's car outside pulling up into Blackhall. What was she doing home at lunchtime? This was the busiest time of the day at Panini's and she never came home then. A minute or so later she drove out again but, horror of horrors, instead of heading back towards Epping she pulled up alongside my Discovery.

I was watching all this through the pub windows, sneaking glimpses with my face tucked behind the window frame. As soon as I saw her car stop alongside mine I knew it meant she'd be coming in the pub. Now, remember, this was a pub I had said I wasn't happy to go in and that she'd practically had to drag me screaming into a short time before. What was I to do?

I did what better and braver men than me have done in the past – I headed for the Gents, the one place I reckoned I'd be safe. I stayed in there for about a quarter of an hour before plucking up the courage to emerge. No sign of Lisa and her car had gone; another close shave. I spent the afternoon getting my 'cover story' ready in preparation for that night.

Sure enough, that evening Lisa asked me, 'Did you go out today?' I told her I'd gone to the garage at lunchtime and filled up with petrol. 'You didn't go to the pub, then?' she asked.

I was ready for this. 'Funny you should mention that, but I did,' I replied. 'I got caught short and whipped in to use their toilet.' Okay, it wasn't the best excuse in the world, but it was all I could come up with.

'Why didn't you just come back here?' she asked.

'I'd locked up and everything and it just seemed easier to run in there,' I replied. Lisa looked at me as though I'd taken leave of my senses, so I decided to go on the offensive. 'What about you?' I said. 'How was your day?'

'A nightmare,' she answered. 'Just as we were getting busy for lunch I realised I'd left my purse with everything in it in the kitchen. I had to come back and collect it.' That explained her surprise daylight visit to the house. It also taught me never to park my car in the pub car park again!

Another complication arising from all this was that Jim at The White Hart would often be pottering around outside the pub and as he was across the road from me, as I've mentioned, he had this habit of waving if he caught sight of me. It was just a friendly gesture on his part, but it always caused me a little bit of panic. If Lisa saw him with his smile and his acknowledgement of me she'd think it a bit strange, to say the least, as it wasn't really the behaviour of a pub landlord who was supposed to hate one of his customers. If he'd been giving me the old two-finger salute that would have been different and it would have fitted in with my story. But this was more like two old buddies getting on famously; it was the last thing I wanted.

I was constantly on guard about letting my secret slip out and I couldn't help thinking of the old wartime motto, 'Careless Talk Costs Lives'. But there were occasions when I was my own worst enemy.

Once I went to the Budgens store in North Weald to get some milk. Lisa was with me and there was a queue at the counter. As I was standing in line the old dear in front got some money out and had her filled-in Lottery card at the ready. I should have kept my mouth shut. I should have talked about the weather if I was going to say something, but no, I just had to go and put my foot in it.

'Are you doing the Lottery?' I asked her. 'I don't know why you bother, I don't know anybody who has ever won, do you?' Lisa was standing alongside me and simply let me carry on babbling away.

The old dear turned to me and said, quick as a flash: 'Well, that's where you're wrong. There's a bloke round here who won £10 million once.'

The danger lights should have been flashing in my brain, but I was hooked on this conversation by now. I was like an alcoholic who knows he mustn't reach for the bottle but just can't stop himself.

'Get away,' I said, 'a friend of yours, is he?'

'No,' she said, 'I wish he was. But I hear he moved his grown-up family into houses he got for them.'

'Good for them,' I said. 'Some people have all the luck.'

That should have been that, but the old dear went on: 'Yes, they had a terrible row over the money, of course, and now they all hate each other. They only talk through lawyers.'

I should have let it rest there. After all, no one in the shop knew it was me she was talking about, least of all the woman herself, and no one knew she was talking complete nonsense. Yet somehow I had this compulsion to defend myself and my family – even though no one knew I was the one under attack.

'I wouldn't believe a word of that,' I said, 'people always start rumours about someone with a bob or two and then they get blown up out of all proportion and you end up hearing a load of nonsense being talked.'

'What are you getting so upset about?' Lisa asked.

'Nothing,' I said. 'It's just that it annoys me when I hear rubbish being talked about Lottery winners.'

'How do you know it's rubbish?' she asked. She'd got me there.

'It always is, isn't it?' I said. There was an awkward moment's silence and then, thankfully, the queue cleared and

I slammed my milk on the counter, paid in double-quick time and headed for the door before anything else was said. I'd realised that not only had I dug a hole for myself, I was digging it deeper by the minute with every remark I made. I wonder if the old dear who was buying her ticket that day has ever realised that the man behind her in the queue was the Lotto winner she was talking about. Perhaps the publicity I later received might have jogged her memory. If it did, I bet she feels a right twit now.

I'm afraid to say that this wasn't the only occasion that I gave in to teasing Lisa without her knowing it, though. Once I'd got problems with the car and Lisa's wasn't available either. With the Porsches locked out of sight it meant that we were temporarily car-less. Nevertheless I met her after work and we had a bite to eat on the outskirts of Epping. As usual, I had to maintain my cover, so we chose a house wine and some of the less expensive dishes on the menu. I even specified tap water rather than the more expensive bottled mineral water when the waitress asked me if we'd like some water to drink; more evidence that I was counting every penny.

It was dark by the time we'd finished eating, so I then had the dilemma of how to get home. I could have rung a pal or a member of the family, but it would have been unfair to expect them to come into Epping and then take us home. I suggested to Lisa that perhaps we should catch a bus and she looked at me as though I was mad. Then I got the number of a mini-cab firm out of my pocket and said something along the lines of, 'Ah well, we'd better push the boat out and get a cab.' I quickly warmed to my theme, though, and added, 'I might need you to chip in, if you don't mind.' Credit where it's due, she agreed with me without any fuss.

Once the cab turned up I told him to take us home and then I kept pointing to the meter and whispering to Lisa, 'These things aren't cheap, are they?' until we arrived home. At the gates to Blackhall, I reached in my pocket and fished out a fiver. 'How much have you got then, Lisa?' I asked and she had to make up the difference. In fact, I think she ended up paying more than me. What she didn't know was that in my other pocket I'd got a wad of £20 notes I'd collected from the bank earlier that day. 'I'll pay you back later,' I said, and just to rub it in I added, 'Make sure you give the driver a decent tip, will you, darling?'

I'd had my little jape, but I thought I might have pushed my luck a bit that night, so as soon as we got indoors I went up to my wardrobe, got some money and handed it over to Lisa in repayment. There is such a thing as over-egging the pudding, after all!

Another time, when we were shopping in London, we went into one of those gentlemen's shops in Jermyn Street, the type with pink shirts and City-gent suits in the window, and I started to browse among the shirts that were laid out in the middle of the floor. It was sale time, so I just looked at the basket that had my size in it. I found one lovely pure cotton number and again I couldn't resist a secret little wind-up with Lisa.

'I can only go up to £20,' I told her, 'and the one I really like is £30.'

Then I looked at her and gave her what I hoped was a rather lost 'little boy' look. Without hesitation she said, 'Go on, have it then, I'll give you the tenner you need.'

I gave her a great big kiss there and then in the middle of the shop and we walked out arm-in-arm with me holding my prized new shirt tightly. I know it was a mean trick to play on her, but it was all part of the process I was putting her – and to a lesser extent myself – through.

I knew in my heart of hearts that I wasn't being such a swine, because when the big day came that I told her of my wealth then the world would be her oyster. I would be pushing the boat out for her big time. All these tenners here and chipping in for Chinese food there would be forgotten when I started buying her whatever she wanted.

One of my biggest worries was being spotted by someone who knew about my Lotto win when I was with Lisa. That meant I needed eyes in the back of my head at times as I went about my daily life. Going into Epping, there were occasions when I must have looked like a character from a spy film: looking over my shoulder as I walked along the road, nervously trying to see through café windows to check if the coast was clear for me to go in. Every shop might have someone from the print-works in there who could turn round and say something like, 'Hello, moneybags!' or 'Here's Mr Millions!'

At least I would be able to recognise them in advance and turn the other way or hightail it for safety. But I also realised there might be acquaintances of mine who had somehow found out about my win without my knowing it. They could let it slip out too and I wouldn't be able to see it coming. Come to that, even total strangers might know me on sight, having being told by someone else …

Talk about becoming paranoid!

9

More Close Shaves

At least when I went to London I would be safe from the panic that sometimes took hold of me in Essex – or so I thought.

Once I took Lisa on one of our window-shopping trips and we found ourselves walking through Soho one sunny winter's afternoon. In my mind I was absent-mindedly fantasising about what it would be like to come to the West End with her when my secret was out and blow thousands on her when, all of a sudden, I saw a suited man striding towards me. To all intents and purposes he looked like one of the Camelot staff who had confirmed my win for me that never-forgotten day. years before. Panic wasn't the word for it. I grabbed Lisa, hissed, 'Come on, let's have a look in here!' and pulled her into the nearest doorway. That wasn't safe enough, the man in the suit might still spot me, so I herded her into the shop itself.

'Why on earth have you brought me into this place?' Lisa said. There was genuine surprise and indignation in her voice and as I turned round I could see why; I had dragged her into an adult bookshop full of porn magazines and videos. There, staring at us from several rows of shelves, was a collection of young men and women with hardly a stitch on in various forms of physical engagement that practically defied description.

I wanted to grab her and take her out immediately, but I was worried that the Lotto man might still be around. 'Oh, I just thought you might like to have a look,' I stammered. 'No, thank you,' said Lisa, who was the only woman in this rather crowded dirty-mac-brigade shop, 'Come on, let's go.' If it had been a delicatessen or an ordinary bookshop I could have browsed for a few minutes, but I couldn't get away with that here. I could hardly start ripping open the covers of the magazines and feign interest in what lay inside; I guess my mistake was walking through Soho in the first place.

I made sure the coast was clear before heading out into the street again. The entire episode can't have lasted more than a minute, but it seemed like an eternity. To this day I'm not sure if the man I saw was from Camelot and, with hindsight, they are probably told never to acknowledge big winners they've met unless they say 'hello' to them first. But it scared the pants off me, that's for sure.

A much closer shave came when we went out for a Chinese meal at a restaurant near Harlow. For once I'd told Lisa that 'the Milky Bars are on me' – I'd be paying. So there was to be no trickery there: we'd just have a pleasant meal and there'd be no worries. I was feeling very relaxed and in a congenial sort of mood. It goes to show why they say that's when you're at your most vulnerable and 'You never hear the bullet that gets you.' That is very nearly what happened to me over my Singapore fried noodles.

We'd ordered our meal; the noodles had arrived, together with chicken in black bean sauce and a lovely portion of duck. The egg-fried rice was delicious and I was just telling Lisa how good it all tasted when the door opened and in walked a familiar face. It was one of my old workmates from the printing factory and alongside him was a rather attractive blonde lady.

I remembered he'd been there the day I had resigned, so he knew that I had millions in the bank – the game could be up for me in a few moments. Of all the gin joints in all the world he had to walk into mine, as the saying goes.

All the delicious Cantonese food suddenly lost its allure, the wine that had flowed pleasingly down my throat a few seconds earlier seemed cheap and acidic. What to do? How could I escape? I couldn't say the food was horrible and storm out, as I'd only just finished saying how good it was. I could say I felt ill, but I'd been on top form a moment ago, so Lisa would suspect something. The only plan I could come up with was the Ostrich Method: stick my head in the sand and hope nothing happened.

I looked at my plate of food and began shovelling it down furiously. My eyes were glued on the plates and dishes in front of me; I was determined to avoid his gaze as he and his companion looked for a table to sit at. It couldn't get any worse, could it? Oh yes, it could!

The restaurant was only half-full, so there were plenty of empty tables, but, with an inevitability that I could have predicted, the waiter beckoned the couple to the table alongside ours. At least they weren't actually touching, but there was a gap of only two or three feet separating us, just enough for the waiters to pass through.

I could only avoid eye contact for so long. I looked at my food, at Lisa, at the menu, at the walls, at every other customer in the place … I looked everywhere except at the man at the table alongside us.

My plate was clean before Lisa had properly started. I even leant over and tried to finish off her portions just so that we could head for the door in next to no time. I asked for the bill while she was still eating and fumbled around for cash to pay it with. The last thing I wanted was to waste agonising minutes paying by credit card and then waiting for it to clear. But as the waiter brought my change, the inevitable happened. My gaze met the man nearby and sure enough, he was looking straight at me. There was recognition in his eyes, I was sure of it. He'd clocked me. What to do?

I thought perhaps I should dash out, telling Lisa I'd see her outside. Perhaps I should use the old trick of heading towards the toilet and then walking straight into the street afterwards. Or I could bluff it out, say hello and make sure he hardly got a word in before exiting stage left.

Before I could make up my mind, a very strange thing happened: he quickly averted his gaze from mine and half-turned his head away. It looked to all intents and purposes as if *he* was the one who didn't want to be recognised.

Thankfully, Lisa had finished by this time and we stood up and started to leave. As we did so I glanced at the attractive, slim blonde sitting with my former workmate. She was a good deal younger than him and, as they say, 'pretty fit'. Then I remembered I'd met the chap's wife once when she came to pick him up from work. She was dark-haired and probably hadn't won too many beauty contests in her life. The shapely lady at the Chinese restaurant table was most definitely not his wife. Perhaps he'd got divorced in the intervening years, but I doubted it. He wasn't the divorcing kind and neither, from what I remembered, was his wife. For once my luck had held: he was obviously out on the town with a woman who was not his wife. The dirty blighter! That meant that of the two of us he was far more nervous about any recognition or talks about 'the good old days' than I was. I didn't want to know him and he definitely didn't want to know me.

I almost let out a cry of relief as Lisa and I walked out into the evening air. Not quite The Great Escape – more like A Close Escape.

Some time later, I took Lisa out in the Range Rover, glanced down and noticed that we were short on petrol. The car might have been in gear but my brains weren't, because I headed straight for a local garage not far from where we were living at Blackhall Farm. It was the place I regularly stopped at before I'd met Lisa because it was so handy and, one way or the other, they knew all about my real circumstances. They may not have known the full details of how I came to be so well-heeled, but they knew enough to be dangerous. The cat could well and truly have escaped from the bag.

Most petrol stations these days are self-service, but this was an exception. That doubled my chance of exposure, as there would be a petrol attendant to deal with as well as whoever was on the cash till.

Unaware of this hazard, I slowly pulled the car onto the garage forecourt and climbed out to meet the young attendant as he strode across to the pump. The radio was on quietly in the Discovery as I asked him to fill the vehicle up with a few gallons of unleaded. We had a brief conversation about the weather, how we were both doing and then the conversation went silent.

Lisa sat in the passenger seat waiting for me to get back in the car when all of a sudden the young mechanic thought he'd restart the conversation. 'Where's the Porsche today then, Joe?' he asked. It's a cliché to say that someone's ears pricked up, but if it has ever happened then this was the day. Lisa had heard his remark and hadn't just taken it on board – she'd allowed it room and lodgings as well.

I paid the bill and climbed back in the driver's seat and gave her a weak smile. I was waiting for the inevitable question – and I didn't have to wait too long.

We hadn't even moved off the forecourt when it came.

'What was all that about, then?' she asked.

'All what about, darling?' I meekly replied, feigning ignorance.

'You and a Porsche, that's what he said.'

I pretended to concentrate on the road as we pulled out and nonchalantly replied as we drove off – with me looking in the rear-view mirror – 'Oh, that.'

'Yes, that,' said Lisa. She wasn't going to let this one go easily.

'It's just a joke he has with me whenever I go in,' I began. There was silence. 'About me having a Porsche ...' I was losing it a bit and realised I mustn't say too much or I'd probably make even more trouble for myself. 'Yeah, he was taking the mickey because I haven't got a Porsche, that's all.'

It wasn't the best of excuses, because his remark could hardly be classified as the funniest joke in history. Lisa gave me a look and I looked at the road ahead. I prayed to myself, 'Lisa let it go, let it go!' and hoped she wouldn't start asking me any more questions. Thankfully she didn't, the danger was over for the time being at least. I made a mental note to double-check that those garages with my Porsches in were still padlocked and the cars were safe from her innocently prying eyes.

One of the biggest 'tests' that I had to go through was when Lisa met Zak for the first time. She's already met Nick and Tina and there were no problems there, but Zak was going to be a completely different kettle of fish. He is a lot more outgoing than the other two and he loves a good old-fashioned chat. Also, he was living a wonderful lifestyle in London when I started going out with Lisa. His home in Fulham was so superbly furnished it had appeared in a couple of design magazines and the *Sunday Times Style* magazine. It was worth over £1 million and it was beautiful.

The problem was that he mustn't let on about his wealth, because that could easily have led to questions about how he'd earned his money and how wealthy I was. I briefed him closely before the big day dawned and as a meeting point we chose the unlikely setting of the Holloway Road in north London. We couldn't go to Fulham, as Zak might have met someone he knew and the ambiance would have been all wrong, which is why we settled for the Holloway Road. I don't know how many of you know that part of north London, but 'exclusive' isn't a word you often hear to describe it. It's okay, sure, but nothing to write home about.

We all travelled in by public transport – me and Lisa from one direction, Zak from another – and met near the tube station there. Normally when I met Zak I would be in my Porsche and he would be in his, but this wasn't going to be one of those days.

Unlike Fulham, the area where we met was hardly bursting with expensive, trendy restaurants. The nearest decent place we could find was a sort of Tex-Mex eatery, so the three of us all sat down to order something.

Zak understood why I was keeping it all secret from Lisa. He's got a lot of genuine friends, but he knew that there might be some others who only wanted to be around him because he had money to spare. So he understood my reticence at telling Lisa the truth. Zak loves to travel and had been around the world, so I had briefed him not to go on about all the fabulous places he'd been to recently when he met Lisa – again, she might have wondered how he managed to do it all. What's more, Zak and I bought each other presents non-stop; he would buy me a watch and I'd buy him all sorts of gifts in return, and if there was any sort of banter about all these gifts then Lisa might twig.

As well as worrying that he might make a slip of the tongue, I was also nervous as to whether he and Lisa would get on. I needn't have worried for a second. They hit it off like a house on fire. They talked non-stop as we munched our way through the cheeseburgers, tacos and refried beans, all washed down with a rather ordinary wine, as Lisa sat there intrigued by his stories of the music business and property development.

At one point, Zak and I excused ourselves and went to the Gents. We were like two teenage girls at a disco talking about a date one of us was on. The conversation went something like this:

Me: 'What do you think of her?'

Zak: I think she's great, just great.'

Me: 'Do you really mean that? You're not just saying that, are you?'

Zak: 'No. She's gorgeous, absolutely gorgeous.'

Me: 'You're not just saying that, are you? You do mean it?

Zak: 'Of course I mean it! She's fantastic. You're lucky to have found her.'

Me: 'We'd better be getting back then, she'll be worried about why we're so long.'

We returned to our table, but it was obvious that Lisa knew we'd been discussing her. She must have felt straightaway that she'd been a 'hit' – you could feel the immediate sense of togetherness we'd all got.

From that day to this, Zak and Lisa have got on really well – they love each other's company. And we no longer have to play at being downbeat at Taco restaurants; we're able to live it up in rather more style now ...

10
The Truth at Last!

I like to be classed as a very romantic guy, which in all honesty I think I am, and at Blackhall we had what we called 'the giant's bed'. It was shaped like a sledge and came from Harrods; you could get lost in the thing, it was so vast. In such a Mills-and-Boon setting you feel obliged to act appropriately, so sometimes in the mornings I'd get up early, go out into the garden, pick a rose from one of the bushes outside and put it in a tiny vase on a tray. Then I'd put a freshly-made cup of tea on a matching saucer alongside some buttered toast, and a little pot of jam alongside the flower, and very carefully go upstairs to bring Lisa breakfast in bed. I thought it was just a lovely way to start the day and she seemed keen on it too.

One day I went through the whole process as usual, carefully carrying it all up the ancient oak stairs to her. Lisa had what I call a blonde wig-piece, it's a hair extension really

I guess, and she had placed it on the pillow as though she had her back to me under the bedding so that all I could see was the top of her 'hair'. Then she plumped up all the pillows and the duvet to make it look as though she was still sleeping. As I tip-toed into the room, for the life of me, I thought she was there still dozing from the night before.

All of a sudden there was this great scream of 'Wah!' and she leapt out at me from the wardrobe where she had been hiding. Up went the tea, the rose, the vase, the toast, the tray, everything … I was so taken by surprise that the lot came down on the floor in one great big mess. Perhaps she'd found out about my money after all and wanted to kill me with fright! Anyway, she didn't get her tea or any of her goodies so that served her right. But it goes to show she's as cranky as me at times.

I still hadn't let on how much money I had, so when we went out with Lisa's sister, Josie, and her husband, Flynn, to maintain the pretence of being hard-up I would have to ask, 'Oh, what type of place are we going to?' – just to make out that I would feel ill at ease in an expensive place and would be pushed to pay my chunk of the bill. So for a spell I'd let the others pick up the tab. I must have done a very good job of this, because I later found out that one night, after her husband had picked up the bill yet again, Josie said to Lisa, 'Joe is a very nice bloke – but I think he's a bit of a tight bastard!' Lisa replied, 'Well, we haven't got what you've got.'

It was actually hard for me to do. In reality, I'm the sort of guy who always puts his hands in his pocket when the bill comes round. If anything, I go too far the other way. So I had to train myself to avoid doing this and curb my natural inclination to be generous.

Oddly enough, I discovered around this time that Lisa was a regular Lottery player. Every Saturday she'd have £5 on Lotto – I'd often ring her up when she was working and she'd say something like, 'Oh I won't be coming straight back, I've got to go and do the Lottery first before I come home.' I would always say, 'You are wasting your money; it's a fix. Have you ever known anyone win it?' I know it was a wind-up and unnecessary, but I only did it, as they say, with the best possible intentions.

I was starting to play the Lottery again around this time. I'd stopped for a long time after I'd won because I thought, 'You greedy bastard, it would be taking the piss if I won again – let someone else have a chance!' Still, I began to think that lightning might strike twice and, to carry on with the metaphors, if you don't buy a ticket you'll never win the raffle.

I hated being apart from Lisa, but I was invited to a wedding in Sri Lanka and I went with my son Nick and his family. I couldn't put it off – it was already paid for, and as a good friend of ours was getting married over there I couldn't not go. I wanted to be there, of course, but the problem was this: I would be leaving Lisa alone at Blackhall for a full two weeks and who knows what she might have found out about me?

I was worried that my secret would come out; I was concerned that she would go over to the pubs and have a meal and get talking to the locals. Then, in the middle of the night, I'd get a telephone call in Sri Lanka and it would be Lisa on the line saying, 'What's this about you being a millionaire?'

I didn't want her being at the house by herself and I insisted that she had someone with her for those two weeks, so her sister Lorraine moved in for that fortnight. Credit where it is due, they did the garden up superbly for me while I was away and Lorraine especially did a great job on it – tidying everything up. I hadn't left any money behind at the house, so Lisa actually paid her £200 for the work she did tidying up the place and, to keep up my image of a guy who didn't have too much money, I didn't pay her when I got back home. (Come to think of it, I *still* haven't paid her!)

I had a great time while I was away, although I couldn't rest and enjoy myself because I missed Lisa so much; we rang each other constantly. During one of the telephone calls Lisa told me her Fiat Punto had packed up. I couldn't resist having another little joke at her expense. Remember, there were a couple of Porsches doing nothing in the garage, but I couldn't let on about that, so I suggested that she walk to the end of a country lane near Blackhall and catch a bus to Epping. It was a good idea, apart from the fact it was a very long lane and it took her over an hour in the depths of an Essex winter to walk to the bus stop. After I'd given her that 'advice' I put the phone down and had a little laugh to myself. I could easily have afforded to have a cab at her beck and call for the entire time I was away. Okay, not the nicest thing in the world to do, but I do like a little joke every now and again.

After a week I couldn't take it any more and I asked her to come out and join me; I didn't care about the cost or arrangements or anything like that. She couldn't do it, though – it's not like hopping on a plane to Spain, where there are loads of flights to different airports every day. There just weren't the flights available that would have got her there in time; she'd practically have to land and immediately turn round and head back home again.

By now, matters were coming to a head. The situation couldn't go on for ever. Every day I was on a knife-edge over whether Lisa would find out the truth. I didn't like the lie I was living and I was unsure of what her reaction would be, should she find out one way or the other.

I'd been very disappointed, 'gutted' as footballers would say, when she had refused my proposal of marriage a little while earlier because she felt it was too early in our relationship. Nevertheless, I was determined to give it a second go.

One evening in March we were all at home. Alfie had gone to bed and Lisa and I were in the living room with *Coronation Street* on television. Now, why that programme was on, I have no idea as neither of us watch it. I'd go further than that: I hate it! It's the most boring programme I have ever seen. But it lives in my memory because of what happened that night.

I'd decided that I would ask Lisa to marry me again. That dreary *Coronation Street* theme tune was just finishing and I spoke up, using the phrase I always used when I wanted to attract her attention and have a serious conversation. 'Lisa,' I announced, 'I have something to tell you.'

'Come out with it, then,' she replied. Now, this got me a little bit wound up. I was beginning to stumble a bit in the conversation and I was almost angry in a way because I really did want to ask her something important.

I calmed down a bit and then said it. I managed to get past my lips the phrase, 'Lisa, will you marry me?' Back came the answer which, if I'm being honest, surprised me.

'Yes,' she said. It was as simple as that.

I am no super-hero, so I'm not afraid to admit it: within moments, I had tears of joy welling up in my eyes. I was actually sniffing. Lisa said, 'Come over here and give me a cuddle.' I told her, 'You have made me the happiest man in the world.' I believe 100 per cent that if you haven't got love in your life then you have nothing. You could have £10 million in the bank (and I should know!), but it really doesn't mean a thing without love.

I had loved her right from the start. And the more I got to know her, the more I loved her. Everything she had done, everything she did, made me more and more certain. She was kind-hearted, among many other things, but she could have been a convicted murderer and I would still have loved her.

Once Lisa had said 'yes', I was on a high. When you get to a high like that, when your emotions are so supercharged, you are so happy you don't want to come down. 'Let's keep rolling the dice,' I thought to myself, and I finally decided to tell her the truth about me and money.

I started to stumble in my speech again; I was struggling to get the words out. Certainly having a verbal battle with myself to get them out in the right order, that is. I began, 'Lisa, I have something else to tell you.'

'What is it, what's the matter?' she answered. I could see it going through her mind that there might be some terrible secret I was about to reveal. Perhaps I was a criminal? Maybe I'd already got a wife I hadn't told her about?

'Lisa,' I continued, 'believe it or not, this is my house. I own it lock, stock and barrel. I won the Lottery and won £10 million.' There, I'd done it. All that torment I'd been enduring ended in a few short words.

Her response: 'Shut up, you're having a laugh!' We'd done a lot together in the time we'd known each other and we often laughed and joked at things – some serious, some silly – and she clearly thought this was one of those occasions. She thought I was simply winding her up.

I told her this wasn't a spoof, that I was being serious, but she wouldn't believe me. If you think about it, no one would blame her for thinking that way, would they? She'd had cheap Chinese meals, paid for food herself and had recently been on a penny-pinching holiday that most people would have needed another break to recover from. And the man who was responsible for all this was now telling her he's worth millions?

Here I was, after months of keeping things from her, months of deceit and evasion, at last coming clean – and not a word of it was accepted as true. Now I was faced with a problem that I hadn't anticipated: how was I to prove my wealth?

Then I thought of a way to do it. In the house was a big, old safe that I kept various documents in. Among them was a copy of the cheque from the National Lottery for the £10 million that had changed my life. My hands were trembling as I opened the safe door and then started to frantically hunt around inside for the cheque. At last I found it and showed it to her.

She was stunned; she was amazed. For the first time, she now realised that I really was a millionaire.

Although I was feeling ecstatic, I was also – and there is no nice way of saying this – shitting myself. She could have exploded and said something like, 'You lying bastard – you've been having me on all the time!' If she had reacted like that it would have been understandable – after all, she was right. I was a liar and I had been having her on – albeit for the best possible motives, in my eyes.

All of a sudden I needed a cuddle again. I was shaking and nervous, and she hugged me and cried at the same time. 'Do you understand why I had to do it?' I asked her, and then explained everything. Lisa went quiet as I told her the reason for it all as the night wore on – the money I had wasted on other women and this feeling I'd had that she might, just might, let my wealth influence her feelings for me if she had known about it from Day One.

By the time I had finished we were in the wee small hours. It was, however, like having a huge weight taken off my back – an even greater relief than the 'weight' that had vanished when I'd won the money. The load had gone; I was free at last.

I had to unburden myself of everything now. I went on, 'Lisa, there are no spiders in the garage, that wasn't the reason I didn't want you to go there.' She gave me one of those looks, as though she was thinking what could be there that I was so ashamed of – six dead bodies, perhaps? So I took her outside, opened the garage doors and showed her the Porsches. As we went in, she was telling me, 'Shut up, you silly git, this has got to be a wind-up.' When she saw the cars inside she simply exclaimed, 'Oh f**k, oh f**k!'

That night went on and on, and on. We sat talking for ages as I finally, fully told her everything and gave her a blow-by-blow account of what had gone wrong before and why I had taken the steps I'd taken. When we finally went to bed we made love; it was wonderful in every sense.

Now I had some catching up to do. I had to start making amends for those cheapskate nights and that dire holiday. And where better to start doing that than at The Ritz? I booked a stay for that weekend at the famous hotel in Mayfair that is synonymous with glamour and sophistication – and big spending.

First, we went into Epping and I bought Lisa a gorgeous black suit that she looked stunning in. Then, that Friday night, I drove to town in one of the Porsches that, thankfully, I no longer had to hide.

The doorman took the keys off me so the car could be parked and I immediately ordered a bottle of the best champagne. Lisa decided to have a shower before dinner and as she was showering I drank the entire bottle myself while I was waiting. I was totally and utterly pissed by the time she came out of the bathroom. It's safe to say that I was very merry as we went down for dinner.

There was an old, fuddy-duddy three-piece band playing, not our sort of music at all. Yet again I said those words to her: 'Lisa, I want to tell you something.' She looked at me and goodness knows what was going through her mind this time.

Then I came out with it, 'Lisa, will you marry me, darling?' I know we'd been through this once before, just a few days earlier, and she'd said 'yes'. And I knew she'd meant it the first time, but I needed to be 100 per cent sure. I know that sounds ridiculous, and it's difficult to explain, but I wanted to go through the proposal and her answer in different conditions just to make sure we were both happy with what lay ahead.

She looked me straight in the eye and I will never forget her reply, 'Only if you do it properly and get down on your hands and knees.'

I wasn't going to be put off; nothing was going to stop me now. It didn't matter one little bit that we were in one of the most famous hotels in the world or that we were surrounded by strangers. My bravado was inspired mainly by my love for Lisa, perhaps aided slightly by that champagne, but there and then, in the dining room at The Ritz in front of all those wealthy, immaculately dressed diners – not to mention the band – I went down on one knee.

It looked like something out of an Edwardian play as I looked into her eyes and asked, once more, 'Lisa, will you marry me?' Everyone in the room was looking at us. I don't know what they thought, and I didn't care; all I cared about was Lisa.

She looked at me, there was a tiny, nerve-wracking pause – because much like myself she likes a little bit of a wind-up on occasions – and then she said, 'Oh, all right then.' There are no words to describe how I felt. Yes, I know she had already agreed a few days earlier, but this was different. This was the confirmation I wanted, the night I needed to convince me that, thankfully, there was no going back.

Now, I'm a normal working-class guy and I don't always feel at home in some surroundings, despite my money. Truth be told, the dining room at The Ritz was one such place. Nothing was going to stop me now, though. I marched up to the leader of the band and asked him, 'Will you announce something for me?'

'Yes, old chap, what is it?' he replied. I told him that I had just asked my girlfriend Lisa to marry me and that she had said 'yes' – and now I wanted him to tell the whole room. He said he'd do it and so, of course, he asked my name.

I didn't want to say common-old-garden Joe, so I told him, 'My name's Joseph.'

I went back to my seat to have my dinner. I had ordered caviar, which I'd never had before – in fact, I wasn't even sure what it looked like. It arrived, with little bits of toast to spread it on, on a massive metal tray covered with ice and a swan also carved out of ice. Just as I was about to tuck into it I heard the announcement from the bandstand: 'Congratulations to Joseph! He has just asked his girlfriend Lisa to marry him and she has said, 'Yes'!'

There was a ripple of applause from all the other diners as I began to tuck into my first course: £135-worth of caviar. I liked it – which, at that price, is a good job really –although I can't remember what else either of us had that night. I simply wanted Lisa to remember that evening for the rest of her life, to have memories that most other couples could only dream of.

We went up to the suite I had taken for the evening at a cost for the night of somewhere in the region of £1,000 and – you guessed it – we made love.

11
Family Approval

Soon afterwards, Lisa gave in her notice. That meant she'd lose her income, about £400 a week, but that wouldn't be a problem. I didn't want her to work any more, there was no need. Lisa and her sister Josie, who was her 'boss' in a way, talked briefly about her staying on and Lisa suggested going in part-time, but Josie said she should leave and stop working completely.

Having spent months pretending to scrimp and save, we now faced a new problem: every time Lisa wanted money she had to come to me for it. Even if it was from a cash machine, I would have to go and do the necessary. I didn't think anything of it though, which wasn't too smart on my part really; I didn't think that Lisa might not be too comfortable with the situation. I simply thought, 'We are going to get married, we are living together. If she needs any money all she has to do is ask.' She had been an independent, wage-earning woman; she had earned her own regular salary and lived off it, financing herself and Alfie. To have that situation change dramatically was bound to cause a few problems, but that never occurred to me.

We even had the occasional little argument about it. If she went shopping at a supermarket I'd have to go with her, and that was awkward. We got around all this at first by me giving her my card and pin number so that she could go to the hole-in-the-wall herself, but there are limitations on this. Even for a millionaire there are daily cash limits for security reasons, so a little later we went to the bank and got Lisa her own chequebook and cards. Later on, after we married, we had a joint account, but even that first step of getting Lisa a card somehow managed to go wrong. I didn't get her one of the mainstream cards like Maestro or MasterCard; the first card I got her was 'dodgy'. Not in the sense that it was invalid and there were no funds to go with it, but because it was one of those that was not universally accepted at a large number of shops, places like supermarkets – in other words, the type of place where you need them most! One day, soon afterwards, she ended up in a Tesco near our home with a great big shopping trolley full of goodies. After queuing up for a while she got to the till but they wouldn't accept the card – it wasn't on the list of plastic that they were happy with. She hadn't got the cash on her and as everyone was waiting there alongside her she was dying of embarrassment. She had to telephone me to drive down quickly and pay for it all. Not a happy bunny!

When she had been earning a weekly salary at Panini's, Lisa would probably buy an item of clothing most weeks. It might be just a simple new top, for example, not necessarily an outfit, but that was one of the reasons she worked – apart from, of course, to bring money in to care for Alfie.

When the financial cat came out of the bag I would hand over my cards and give her the pin number, thinking that was that sorted. I suppose my attitude to money is best summed up by how I felt when I first won. The men from the bank were sitting down telling me, 'There is fifteen per cent on this and two per cent on that' and, 'There are TESSAs that you can buy' and so on and so forth. I could not give a shit about all that at the time. My attitude was that I had a son, Nick, who had a banking background, and he was as honest as the day is long, so he could look after all that for me.

By the time Lisa moved in with me, Nick was coming round once a month, effectively in the role of my 'bank manager'. He would tell me where to sign and I wouldn't even read the paperwork, I'd just slap my signature on bills, letters to the bank, everything. I wasn't worried about it, for the obvious reason that I trusted him totally.

After Lisa moved in, she asked me, 'Can't you do all that yourself? Shouldn't you be sorting that out on your own?'

'Not really, because he is more educated in that field.' I told her. 'And, to be honest, I am not really interested.'

She replied, 'Well, I think we should start doing it ourselves.'

I had a beautiful office at home with the safe in and I showed her some of the papers in there. As I showed them to

Lisa she began asking me questions: 'What is that paper for?' 'What is this document for?' and I became immensely frustrated – and embarrassed – because I simply did not know.

Understandably, she pressed me on this: 'But you must know, surely?' She felt that, in a way, I was hiding things from her – but I wasn't. My view was: 'I've worked hard all my life, I don't want to know what they are all for, I don't want to be bothered with things like this now – I don't need to any more.' I should add that all this has changed and these days we keep a much more careful eye on our finances than we did back then. It caused us a few arguments, though.

There was something else that aroused friction between the two of us. Of course we had money to burn; of course we were madly in love – but love and cash don't mean you can't have disagreements, as we soon found out.

The closeness I had with my daughter Tina was a different kind of love: Tina kept an eye on me and Lisa kept an eye on Tina. I loved them both, so I had to strike a balance between these two different types of the same emotion. Once I was having a row with Lisa and I lost my temper when she said to me, 'You think more of Tina than you do of me!' So – and this was a foolish thing to do – I immediately picked up the telephone and called Tina. I said to her, with Lisa standing there listening, that to make things clear, 'Lisa is my Number One now.'

Now, Tina is married and her husband is Number One to her, but it was an ill-advised remark spoken in temper – something you should never really do. It was disloyal of me and I shouldn't have said it. Lisa and my children didn't see eye-to-eye for a period after that, but they made it up fairly soon afterwards.

I hadn't told any of my family that I was planning to propose, so it was only after that magical night at The Ritz and Lisa definitely saying 'yes' that I got round to telling them.

I couldn't wait to tell people, to let the world know. A few days after that night, Lisa and I were driving along Epping High Street and I was talking on the car-phone to Nick's wife Dawn. Obviously they did not realise that Lisa was in the car. I took the plunge and told them, 'I have asked Lisa to marry me.' The phone went quiet. So I decided to phone Nick at his home nearby and Dawn answered. I said, 'Say something Dawn, say something.' And she replied, 'Well, it's all a bit too soon.'

I guess they thought that because of the fiasco I had been through with the other women it might be a case of 'Here we go again'. In a way, I could understand them feeling like that. The thought might have gone through their heads that Lisa was after their dad's money. I knew she wasn't, but they had not known her long enough, and certainly didn't know her well enough, not to draw a conclusion like that.

Nick and Tina didn't go overboard with their congratulations, but at the same time they weren't trying to discourage me. It was not a negative reaction on their part, it was a positive one. At the same time you would have to call it positive with a small 'p'. The truth is, if they had said to me,

'Don't do it, Dad' or, more realistically, 'Don't do it yet, Dad, wait a year or so,' I would not have taken a blind bit of notice. Perhaps they knew this. When I decide to do something, I do it no matter what other people might say. Whether I am right or wrong I go straight ahead – although this time I *knew* I was in the right.

I met Lisa's mother, Shirley, and her father, Joe, around this time – lovely, lovely people. Her father looked at me in what can best be called a subdued sort of way, obviously because I was going out with his daughter. She was still married and her first husband, Billy, was established with the family; I wasn't. We soon got together, however, and I was dead straight with him and assured him I loved his daughter and would look after her. I told him all the things any worried father would want to hear, but I was totally honest with him in what I was saying. Mind you, when Lisa told her mum and dad that we were going to get married and that I was a Lottery winner, her father said, 'Good for you, girl! He seems a nice bloke, and he's got money.' I've got to mention it because it hurt me big-time when I heard that. That put me on a downer. Money wasn't a factor in our relationship – it was love. But he'd always been an 'earner', he'd brought money in to look after his family, so I guess it was a way of saying that his daughter would now be well looked after. But it did upset me when I heard that and I would be lying if I said otherwise.

There was another difficulty ahead. Lisa's brother John was very protective of her in the way that some brothers are and

Lisa told me, 'Look, I don't know how he is going to take it. He might punch you in the nose and say, "What are you doing with my sister?" or whatever.' She was particularly worried about this. I wasn't worried or afraid, for the simple reason that I knew what I wanted and if there were to be any consequences of my action, then they would just have to happen whatever they might be and whatever effect they had on me. I was extremely philosophical about it all, even though in their younger days her brother had been especially protective – if anyone moved in on Lisa and made a play he would challenge them.

Fortunately, when we eventually met, we got on fine. He even commented, for some reason, that he thought I looked like Tony Curtis. I presume he didn't mean like Tony Curtis in drag in *Some Like it Hot*, but in his matinee-idol days! But it was a hurdle and I'm glad we faced it and got over it.

Of course, Lisa also had to finalise her split with Billy. They had been apart for some time and Billy had already said that he wanted a divorce, so she told him she had met me after they split up, was planning on getting re-married and now wanted a divorce too. So that was that underway.

There is one thing that I haven't mentioned yet: the age difference between Lisa and myself. She is 23 years younger than me, but it didn't make the slightest difference to us. For a start, I am not one of this guys you see who automatically just fall for the younger woman. If a woman is 96 and you fall in love with her, that's that – it's happened. It didn't bother Lisa either that I was old enough to be her father – it just wasn't a factor. I like to think that I was in okay condition anyway and I didn't look bad for my age. It may sound a bit of a vain thing to say, but I have always looked after my appearance, so why not?

One thing that was for sure – I certainly didn't feel like a man old enough to be Lisa's dad!

12
Preparing for the Big Day

The magical part was about to begin. The lies had come to an end and I could, at last, be open with Lisa about everything. And one of the key parts of all this – perhaps *the* key part – was that at last the gloves could come off when it came to spending. After the months of watching every penny I spent in case I unwittingly gave the game away, I could now dust off my cheque book, polish up my credit card and unfurl a thick wad of crispy new bank notes in front of Lisa without her thinking I'd taken leave of my senses. Goodbye Mr Scrooge, hello Big Spender!

Out there in that great big wide world of consumerism lay countless shops and stores itching for customers like Lisa and myself to saunter through their automatically opening front doors. I like to think we did not fall into a 'more-money-than-sense' bracket of clientele, but we could definitely be called 'shoppers-with-attitude'. The cash registers and credit card machines beckoned, and who were we to resist their siren call?

First stop, the West End of London. What you must remember is that this was the first shopping trip we'd been on since I'd told Lisa of my win. The last occasion we'd been out on one together – when she still thought I was hard-pressed for cash – we'd gone to the Lakeside Shopping Centre, just off the M25. It's very nice, I'm not knocking it, but if I was to make a football comparison, we were about to step up from a Sunday morning pub football league to the World Cup Finals. Just to emphasise the point, we didn't even buy anything on that final Lakeside trip, we just window-shopped. That was the sort of life we led then, dictated by the budget we were living on because of my deception.

This time, though, Lakeside and the M25 were nowhere in sight. And traffic jams weren't caused by road-works near the Dartford Tunnel, more likely by chauffeurs unable to manoeuvre the limousines of the fabulously wealthy around the tight corners and one-way streets of London W1. It was Mayfair for us.

The first stop was Burberry in New Bond Street. Its two giant flags – a Union Jack and the Cross of St George – flapped from dark mahogany poles alongside the impressive entrance, above the immaculately trimmed tiny trees in their perfectly proportioned wooden tubs. Burberry is famous for its range of rainwear and scarves that have kept the gentry dry and warm since the days 21-year-old draper's apprentice Thomas Burberry opened his first shop in unprepossessing

Basingstoke in Victorian times. There can't have been many stranger sights that have greeted their staff in the century and half since than yours truly trying to persuade my wife-to-be to choose a raincoat.

As soon as Lisa looked at anything, let alone touched it, I'd say to her, 'Try it on, go on, try it on!' She gently put her hand against a cream mac, just running her fingers along it really, and I immediately suggested she put it on to see what it looked like on and how well it fitted. Lisa said, 'No, no. I don't want to try it on.' I kept on urging her and she said, 'I'm only looking.' That wasn't going to put me off though, was it? I was a man with a mission. I went straight up the woman assistant and said, 'Have you got one in her size?' Off she scurried to get it and within moments Lisa was walking around in the raincoat with its distinctive check-patterned lining and looking at herself none too happily in the mirror. All the while she kept saying, 'No, I don't want it.'

She took it off and her final words to me on the subject were, 'Joe, I really don't want it.' You couldn't wish for clearer instructions than that, could you? The lady had made up her mind and that was definitely that. Oh no, it wasn't.

The next time she turned round to look at me, there I was holding an unmistakable Burberry bag – and inside it was, of course, the raincoat.

The reason I did that, bought it against her wishes, was simply that I thought she being polite. I was assuming that she just didn't want to be rude, or what she wrongly perceived to be rude, by accepting some expensive gift from me

149

straightaway. In order to buy something like that just a few days earlier, Lisa would have had to have saved from her salary for weeks. I thought perhaps that in some way that factor was affecting her decision. I bought it for her because I thought she liked it, and the £500 it cost wasn't going to bankrupt me, after all. She did wear it on a few occasions afterwards, but it turned out that she wasn't being polite; there was no subconscious rejection or embarrassment on her part. There was no hidden agenda either – there never *is* with her. She didn't want it because she simply didn't like it! It was as straightforward as that.

Then it was across the road to Old Bond Street. This time I didn't have to do too much persuading – we were heading for Gucci. Obviously, their goods – clothes, shoes and famous leather accessories – were more to Lisa's taste than Burberry, as her eyes lit up with pleasure when she saw the items they had. But it was exciting for me too. This was what I had been waiting for, the chance to spend some of my money on her and make her happy. It was my dream come true. I had wanted to shower her with goodies ever since I had first met her and now I had my chance.

Lisa was quite restrained, really. But she loved a leather handbag, so that was a cert for the shopping trolley – if Gucci had such a thing, that is. Next came a purse that matched nicely with the bag and, while we were at it, a make-up bag for all the beautiful make-up that I would soon be getting her. Before too long we had taken care of £2,000-worth of goods.

Next stop, Harvey Nicks in Knightsbridge. We probably

bought a few more goodies there, although I can't remember what they were now.

By this time we were peckish – well, who wouldn't be after all that hard shopping? So it was back to Bond Street and a spot of lunch at a table outside one of the delightful restaurants in the area. For months we had looked down the right-hand side of menus, taking note of the prices, before we ate. This time we just chose what we fancied – and no more house wine, thank you very much.

I was deliriously happy; I just wanted to give my baby everything that she wanted. If she had a suit, then I would say to her, 'Go on, get a nice bag to match!' If we were going out to an event we'd get a new outfit for the occasion. We didn't always shop up in the West End; often, we were a lot nearer to home. They loved us in Epping High Street too, I can tell you, which isn't all that surprising as we'd often get two of everything, just to be on the safe side. Even now when we walk down Epping High Street, it's, 'Hello Joe, hello Lisa, how are you?'

One of the good things about our relationship was that our two families had met and got on well. We'd often go out with Lisa's sister, Josie, and her husband, Flynn. Flynn isn't short of a bob or two and they were used to going to nice places, so we'd often go out and eat with them. They like what we like: nice, trendy clothes and good, comfortable restaurants with top-class food.

We'd also see my son Zak and his boyfriend. He'd got two houses on the go by then – one in Fulham and one in

Blackheath – and all those visits to him invariably turned into shopping trips. We'd always be buying bottles of champagne every time we saw him.

As well as starting on a spending spree, I wanted to make amends for that awful holiday we'd had in Tenerife a short time before. Many people would have been put off the island for good by our experience, but I knew it was just a bad week in a nightmare location. The island itself is smashing, with a lovely all-year round mild climate, and I've always been fond of the place, even though it has become commercialised in recent times. It holds special memories for me, as I spent a lot of time there when I was younger.

I went into my local travel agent in Epping and asked them what decent places they could offer in Tenerife. I could have picked a luxury hotel if I'd wanted, but I was actually more concerned with just getting away and having a nice break rather than pushing the boat out at a luxury place. We chose a pleasant hotel and, at least on this visit to the island, we had proper rooms with comfortable beds – and not a cockroach in sight. There were undoubtedly better, more opulent places to go, but it was the break that was important this time, not so much the standard of the place we were staying at – as long as it wasn't like the terrible place we'd been lumbered with before.

We took Lisa's lad Alfie with us this time and drove around the island, went on a cable car and messed around in the sea on jet skis. The hotel was a four-star and the entire week cost about £3,000. Not a small sum, true, but one that a lot of people would spend on a holiday for three. While we were there, if there was anything we saw in a shop window that we liked, we'd just buy it. On one occasion we bought Lisa a diamond bracelet; and we also got some smashing clothes for Alfie.

Just think, four months earlier we'd been on a holiday nightmare, afraid to eat in our hotel and ashamed even to admit where we were staying.

Every night on our 'real' holiday we would go out and have a drink. Los Cristianos was still our favourite area to visit, either in a taxi or just by strolling there, and this time we weren't embarrassed to reveal which hotel we were booked into. There are some marvellous places to eat in the town and we'd enjoy lobster washed down with champagne or the best French wine. This was more like it! The memories of that terrible holiday just a short time earlier were drowned by the wonderful time we were now having – and the odd bottle or two of champagne we uncorked. Later, we would put Alfie to bed and – as we are wont to do – make love.

It was during one of these evenings that we discovered 'our band'. We saw them in a bar, one of those trendy places where different acts come on and perform, and thought they were fantastic. We had been thinking about having a pre-wedding party, about a month before the actual wedding ceremony, either in a hotel or somewhere else, although we eventually resolved to have it at Tilegate Farm. I asked Lisa if she would like to have this band play at the party, and she agreed she would. There were five or six guys in the band – English,

American and Indian – and they played *Blues Brothers*-style music. They had a look that was instantly recognisable from the hit film of a few years earlier, starring Dan Aykroyd and John Belushi; the dark suits, glasses and trilby hats. They weren't tacky or anything like that, no way. They were great – exciting music and a terrific live performance. I loved the trumpet, the guitars, everything about them. We even took a video of one of their performances so we would have a record of it back home.

During their break one night I got talking to the leader of the band and outlined what we wanted to do. We told him that we were due to be married and we would like them to come over to England and play at a bash in the marquee we were having. He gave me a dubious look and said, 'Sure, all right,' but I could tell he was thinking it wasn't going to happen. He probably assumed that I was just another tourist enjoying a night out and knocking back a few beers with ideas that would never come to fruition.

So we had a meeting with the guys in their hotel the next day, a Sunday, and ran through it all. They still weren't convinced and I'm sure they only felt it was 'on' when we booked flights for the lot of them and accommodation in a hotel near our home. At last the penny must have dropped and they realised they had a great gig coming their way.

Lisa had always spent a lot of time with her sister Josie before we met, but after agreeing to marry me and stopping work she wasn't seeing as much of her. I know that to begin with life was a bit of a whirlwind and she missed seeing Josie, because she would either be at home with me or out on shopping trips.

But they made up for it by planning the nuptials. They got together and decided it would be great to have a fairytale wedding. The actual ceremony was to be abroad – I'll get to that later – so one of the best ways to have our friends and family celebrate with us was to have a marquee in the grounds of Tilegate Farm and have about 150 people come along to the bash. We are talking September 2001 by now, and September is a beautiful time of year in that part of the country. I know Essex has this image, practically a cliché, of girls in white stilettos being chased around the disco floor by oversexed Del-Boys, but it is also one of the most lovely counties you could find. Tilegate Farm, for example, is very near the M11 and not far from towns like Harlow and Chelmsford, which don't have great reputations for their scenic attractions. Yet when you arrive in the tiny hamlet of High Laver, where the farm is, you could be miles from the nearest town or busy road. It seems as if you have been transported into a real-life version of *The Darling Buds of May*. And September, as summer draws to a close, is when the area is arguably at its best.

Anyway, the girls and I went to a company near Ongar who specialised in these sumptuous wedding bashes and big outdoor parties. We went through their entire catalogue and the tent we finally chose was the bees' knees. The floor was made of solid wood, there were flashing lights all around the marquee, inside and out, a proper stage for the band to perform on and even the toilets were the best available: gold-coloured fittings and lovely porcelain sinks that were better than a lot of people have in their own homes.

I wanted to have an engagement, but Lisa disagreed. Her view was that we'd both been married before, so there was no need to go through a rather long, drawn-out period of engagement. She felt so strongly about it that she didn't even want an engagement ring – quite a result, financially!

That didn't stop us doing some of the necessary things that a man and a woman planning to say 'I do' have to get on with. One of the main things any groom has to choose is what to wear on his big day. It wasn't going to be in an English country church or anything like that, so morning coat with tails was out for starters – Moss Bros wasn't going to be seeing me in a hurry. Instead, we decided to go and buy me a suit … and Josie came too, of course.

We must have covered the whole of London. I have never met a woman like Josie. One minute she was frantically looking through everything on a rack and the next she would suddenly turn around and say, 'Right, next shop!' Then she was off like an express train. We went everywhere: Harrods, Selfridges, Gucci and some other places I can't remember – they all blurred into one after a while. You name it, though, we went there. If there was an Olympic contest to see how many shops you can go in and out of in the shortest space of time, then Josie would have won the gold medal.

On and on we went looking for a suit for me. It didn't

matter how famous the stores were, how exclusive the boutiques were, none of it was right in Josie's book. I'd try something on and she'd say, 'No, that's no good' and so I'd try something else on. She'd say straightaway, 'No, that's no good either.' It was a nightmare. It was like travelling in a car at 200mph with a driver who was accelerating all the time.

After going in and out of what seemed like every store in London, guess where I ended up? A boutique in Buckhurst Hill in Essex, that's where! It was, it must be said, a very nice boutique – but I still had to have the trousers taken up on the suit that I – and 'the committee' – chose.

I must say, it was a cracking suit; I still wear the jacket a lot. So it should be mind, it was made by Dolce and Gabbana, the Milan-based designers who make clothes for people like Madonna and Kylie Minogue. It was lightweight and fitted me to a tee. I'd get a lot of use out of too. Not only for the party but for the wedding we were planning a little while later too.

The cost? Not much change out of £1,500. The colour? A rather fetching baby blue. Well, I did say I wasn't going to go to Moss Bros, didn't I?

That was me sorted. Now for Lisa …

13

The Party of the Year

If getting me togged up for the wedding bash wasn't complicated enough, getting Lisa's outfit was a military operation comparable only to something like the D-Day Landings. The troops in this particular case consisted of Lisa, her sister Josie again, Tina and Dawn. It was, from all accounts, a nightmare … in the nicest possible sense, of course.

I say, 'from all accounts', as I wasn't one of the group – thank goodness. I stayed at home, out of harm's way. Nothing gave or gives me greater pleasure than buying for Lisa, but this time I felt my presence would probably only complicate matters, so the girls might as well get on with it by themselves. I know every cough and splutter of what happened, though, as I received a blow-by-blow account when they returned, exhausted but triumphant, their mission accomplished.

Tina and Dawn might have thought they were just going

on a shopping trip. Quite an important one, of course, but a shopping trip nevertheless. Instead they found themselves part of this unyielding invasion force that landed on the West End one day.

Shop assistants in stores around such an exclusive part of town are pretty used to unusual customers. Forget those pop stars and oil-rich Arab ladies, though – I don't think any one of them can have encountered the likes of those Essex girls arriving on their mission.

Josie was at the head of the group, motoring as usual at her 100mph-and-above cruising speed. She would poke her head in a boutique, have a quick look, decide it wasn't the right place and practically be off and running by the time the rest of the girls turned up. Lisa was leaving all the decisions about which shops to go to, and which dress to go for, to Josie. Joking apart, Josie was invaluable in that she has really good taste and she knows exactly what she wants. The trouble with that is, it also means that she knows exactly what she *doesn't* want, so a lot of potential contenders for Lisa's dress – some of them created by some of the most famous designers in the world – were examined and dismissed in moments.

It seemed there wasn't a dress shop in the West End, Belgravia or Knightsbridge that the gang didn't visit. They were in and out of Harrods before you could say, 'Mohamed Al Fayed.' It's a good job the owner himself wasn't knocking around that day, otherwise Josie would probably have had him showing them a selection of dresses and ordering him to get them a taxi to the next store.

The hunt finally came to an end at Alberta Ferretti's store in Sloane Street, Knightsbridge – just a few hundred yards from Harrods, as it turned out. I say 'ended', but the truth of the matter is that it began there too. As always on days like this, it had been the very first place the girls had gone into a few hours earlier – although it seemed like an eternity before by the time the big decision was made.

A quick browse on the Internet will reveal that Ms Ferretti is known as a 'master of ephemeral style, she gives her creations an ultra-feminine injection – a column of pleating on a fluttery goddess gown' and that she is known for her 'decisive cuts, luxurious fabrics, beautiful construction and soft silhouettes'. Crikey! With all that going for her, what took the girls so long to decide it was the place for them? Ferretti is also favoured by actresses such as Sarah Jessica Parker and Uma Thurman. To my way of thinking, it was only fitting that my Lisa should wear clothes similar to women who have their names up in lights, because in my book she is a bigger star than anyone in Hollywood.

Lisa, Josie and the gang chose a cream silk number flowing down to the floor with a slip underneath it. It had a netted top and was covered in pearls and diamanté. Very classy, very elegant and very suitable for Lisa's wonderful slim shape. There wasn't much change out of £2,500 – which, although not cheap by any means, is actually quite reasonable for a dress for such an important occasion and from such a famous designer. She could have spent a lot more if she had wanted; Lisa had carte blanche to fork out whatever it took to get the dress that made her happy, but the Ferretti one suited her fine and she was more than happy to settle for it. And Josie liked it too.

By the time the question of the dress was resolved, Lisa had become used to travelling in style. She drove a Fiat Punto when I first met her and that was her car throughout the time I was keeping my wealth secret. She would park it outside our home near the garages where the Porsches were secretly stashed and I would look at it and think to myself, 'One day, one day …' After my secret was divulged, I decided she deserved something a step up the motoring ladder. She couldn't decide what sort of car to choose for herself, so I told her to use one of the Porsches – yes, my other car really *was* a Porsche – or the Range Rover whenever she wanted.

The instant she got behind the wheel of the Porsche, she loved it. Talk about taking to something like a duck to water, it was just right for her! The very first time she drove it was when she came out with me while I was dropping one of the other cars off for a service. It takes some getting used to, driving a car like that. I'm not talking about the clutch or the gears or anything as trivial as that, though. I'm talking about the reaction it creates in other road users and pedestrians. Lisa suddenly noticed that people would be looking at her and the car when they pulled up at traffic lights and found herself thinking, 'God, all those people think that I'm some poor little rich girl!'

She used to have this thing when she had her Punto of noticing young girls alongside her in, say, flash Audis, and thinking, 'Bloody hell!' Well, now the tables were turned. She was in the Porsche seeing young girls in their Fiestas and thinking to herself, 'I used to do this, I used to be this.' The truth of the matter is, of course, the real person doesn't change one iota just because you're behind the wheel of an expensive motor rather than a run-of-the-mill set of wheels.

Another thing: you have to get used to boy racers pulling up alongside and giving you and the car the eye. They'd rev up as if they were on the starting grid at Brands Hatch and I'd think, 'Don't even go there, mate, don't even consider it.' It didn't matter how hard they put their foot down on the gas, they didn't stand a chance against the Porsche. Most of the time I'd let the idiots roar away but a couple of times I lost it and thought, 'Vroom vroom, here we go' and within seconds I'd put them in their place. It's a man thing, isn't it?

It was everyone's 'thing', come the day of our pre-wedding bash. Lisa had got her outfit and I had got mine, but that was only the start of it. The day itself cost £100,000. Yes, it is a lot of money, even by my standards and by the money I'd gone through since that crazy £10 million win; it was a lot of cash to spend on one fleeting occasion. Put yourself in my position, though. If you had worked over a number of years and gradually amassed an amount able to cover such a bill you would no doubt think long and hard before spending a six-figure sum in one single day on something that is just a memory twenty-four hours later. It's not as though we are talking about a house or a car, which is tangible and has a cash value even after you've bought it. But I'd come from nothing and I wanted to splash out. To put it in its most crude terms: I didn't give a shit; I wanted it and I was going to have it. It might look cold when you put it that way, but I reckoned that I deserved to be in this position and make the decisions that I did, given the hard times I'd been through for a large portion of my life.

I'll tell you something about that party – it was worth every single penny. I thought it at the time and I still think it. Even now, years later, the memory of it is still with Lisa and me. We've got photos and film too, but it is the sheer glow of happiness that it brings when we recall that day that means the most.

Yet again it was Lisa who was the brains behind organising everything – together with sister Josie, of course. As always, the girls chose the best. They had liaised with the marquee company, who in turn put them in touch with the caterers, who had actually cooked for the Queen on the Royal Yacht *Britannia*. Just think of that: Joe from the printers and Lisa from the café having Her Majesty's finest preparing our food for us! A few months earlier I'd been tucking into that breakfast special at Panini's and now it was nosh fit for HRH. And what food it was! You could describe it as a buffet, and in one sense you'd be right in that it was mainly cold foods served from long tables. It was, however, a buffet most people will never have the privilege of tucking into in their lives.

Poached and smoked salmon, beautiful organic chicken,

thin pieces of breaded escallops of veal, chunks of rib of rare beef cooked to perfection ... Desserts of whipped cream and chocolate guaranteed to pile on the pounds for even the most careful eater. Local fresh fruit and vegetables. All this washed down with a selection of superb French and Italian red and white wines, not to mention vintage French Bollinger champagne. Not a bottle of Cava or any sparkling white wine in sight! Even the lager – and there was plenty of that too – was the best German Pilsner. Everyone ate and ate until they could hardly move. Well, not everyone. There were two people who didn't touch a morsel: Lisa and me. We were too busy or nervous or excited, or a combination of all three, to pick up a plate and join the queue.

And after everyone had been dined and wined, they could always wander over to another corner of the garden for a 'top-up' – we had an entire pig roasting on a giant spit there.

My son Nick made the best-man speech. It was very funny and very affectionate and it went down a storm with all the guests. Then I introduced the band. That may not sound too exciting, but I had always harboured this ambition to introduce a band, a bit like a combination of the host of *Sunday Night at the Palladium* and the DJs from *Top of the Pops*. I'd say, 'And on lead guitar we have ...', 'Meet your drummer tonight, he is ...' and so on. It was probably a bit too late for me to start a new career in show business, but for just that one night it was perfection.

As if all that wasn't enough, the entire marquee was festooned with flowers; the scent and the array of colours was staggering. It was the sort of display that would put the Chelsea Flower Show to shame.

This was the day I had dreamt of since virtually the first moment I set eyes on Lisa. Through all those months of deceit and lies, I had hoped that it might end like this. I couldn't believe it went so well – even better than I had hoped it would be. Life is life and all I wanted to do was to give my Lisa the best. Dead simple, really …

You ask some people what they did for their wedding and they will say they had a quiet 'do' and then went to Southend for a honeymoon, or something like that. Now I'm not knocking that, not knocking it for one minute. The difference is I was in the fortunate position of being able to do things differently – I could go down a more exotic road.

I had proposed in The Ritz, thrown a party fit – literally – for a queen and we would soon be going on an astonishing honeymoon.

Some people might have a guilt trip about spending so much on this caviar lifestyle, but not me. Why should I? Yes, it crossed my mind on occasions that the money I had might be spent, how shall I put it, more wisely, but I was sure – and still am – that I was doing the right thing. I gave all my children a large sum each and I was free to do what I wanted with the remainder. I'd had hard times in my life and there had been occasions when I'd gone to bed exhausted and beaten. I'd heave myself onto the mattress and think, 'If this is life, then what's the point?' It had even reached the point where I thought it would be better if I didn't wake up – it really was as bad as that. I know I'm not alone in having thoughts like those; there must be millions of people on the planet who share them at one time or another, but that doesn't make them any easier to cope with, does it?

Now everything was in my favour. I was being repaid for those bad times, not double but tenfold. It balanced it all out, so why should I feel guilty?

I think somebody up there gave me a break. And a truly lovely break it was too.

14

Trouble in Paradise

Where to get married is a problem facing virtually every couple who are planning on taking the giant step of matrimony; we were no different. All right, the circumstances might have been better for us than for the vast majority of men and women, in that our budget was no problem – well, the sky was the limit, really – but the dilemma still remained: where should we go to say 'I do'?

We were lucky – we ended up choosing Paradise. As the Good Book reminds us, however, even in Paradise trouble is waiting to strike. We were to find that out during the most eventful wedding and honeymoon that anyone could ever have dreamt of. Still, I'm getting ahead of myself. First of all, with all the globe to stick a pin in, how did we come to select the place where we would start our married life?

As you've probably gathered by now, Lisa's sister Josie plays a large part in our lives and she's the one we have to thank for

169

finding that tiny, gorgeous spot on the map where we were destined to end up. We'd spent months thinking about hiring a villa somewhere, staying at a luxury hotel, possibly a cruise, a train journey across a continent – and rejected the lot. There were adventure holidays, romantic specials, back-to-nature trekking, luxury getaway-from-it all escapes … You name it, we thought of it. There can't have been a boutique hotel or designer-chic resort anywhere on the globe that didn't come under our microscope; they were all discussed and discarded. The brochures lay scattered around the house and we regularly pored through the travel supplements in the more upmarket newspapers for ideas, all without success. In a strange way – not that I'm being hypocritical by complaining, I hasten to add – our wealth meant that we were spoilt for choice. Other couples know their spending limit, so simply look to find somewhere that falls within it. Easy as pie. We had a different problem. Unlike them, we weren't constrained by budget, so nothing could be ruled out; it made the choice larger and even more difficult. I'd got so many things wrong in my life that I was determined this one was going to be right on the button. Over to Josie.

Josie likes to read about the rich and famous – we all do, if only we'd admit it – so one day she was perusing *OK!* magazine, the glitz and glamour guide to the goings-on of the Beautiful People, and noticed an article about Princess Stephanie of Monaco on holiday in Mauritius. Princess Stephanie, for those who don't know, is the daughter of the late film star Grace Kelly. She also happens to be the kind of royal who makes our lot at Buckingham Palace look like members of the Salvation Army. She's been a would-be pop singer, a swimwear designer, fashion model and part-time waitress. The men in her life have included movie hunk Rob Lowe, a con-man who served time for fraud, a former gendarme, a trapeze artist and a Corsican barman among others. More of that young lady later.

It wasn't just the Princess's activities that caught eagle-eyed Josie's attention. No, it was the beauty of the island she was on and, more importantly, the opulent style of the hotel she was staying at.

The One & Only Le Saint Géran is one of the world's great hotels. For all I know, it could be the best – it certainly is in my book. It takes its name partly from the tiny, exclusive group of hotels – the 'One & Only' – to which it belongs and partly from the East India Company ship *Saint Géran*, which was wrecked on the coast nearby in 1744. History lesson over for the day, on with the story.

Josie spotted its potential and suggested it to us as a perfect spot to get married. She has given us some good advice over the years, but this was one of the best suggestions even she has ever come up with. She talked us into it, although we didn't take all that much persuading.

Next stop was our usual travel agent in Epping High Street. We should have been put on his Christmas card list by this time for all the custom we were bringing him. His little eyes practically lit up as we came through the door yet again and they went even wider when we said where we wanted to go and why. 'A wedding package to one of the world's great hotels? Expense isn't an issue? Certainly sir, no problem.' It was a bit like walking into a car showroom and saying, 'I want the best car you've got and I don't care how much it costs.' It's astonishing how good the service you receive is when people know where you're coming from on matters like that!

So the holiday was booked through the travel operators Kuoni. They do some wonderful breaks but this was one of the best they could come up with, even by their pretty high standards. All done, no pain and a lot of gain. Two weeks at this renowned hotel with the wedding taking place in the second week. The delay before the actual ceremony meant we would have plenty of time to recover from the flight, sort out various matters of administration linked to the wedding and perhaps even top up our tans by the pool or on the beach before the big day. Nothing could be simpler, could it?

Over 200 years ago, acclaimed Scottish poet Mr Robert Burns noted that the best-laid plans of mice and men often go astray. He could have been talking about me and Lisa. Perhaps he foresaw what effect airports and motorways were to have on us all.

In this day and age every air traveller in the world knows the first criterion on any modern holiday – especially the holiday of a lifetime, when you are going to get married – is not to miss the plane. The fairly straightforward task of reaching an airport can be horrendous. Getting through the place, check-in, customs, security and boarding is invariably a nightmare.

Just to make matters worse, I am one of those people who insist on being at an airport a long time before the plane takes off, a long time before check-in opens, a long time before …well, let's just say I like to get there early. I love to calmly get the bags sorted and then have a relaxing cup of coffee while the rest of the travellers scurry around at coronary-inducing speed in a panic.

Unfortunately, the same gene can't be floating around in Lisa's system. I'm not suggesting that she leaves it to the last minute, but she waits for her name to be called, and she doesn't have the same compulsion – all right, panic – that I have.

This particular departure day, I'd got it all worked out that we must leave home at 2pm to get to Gatwick on time for the flight. The expensive array of Italian leather luggage packed to overflowing with designer gear lay waiting in the hall, the antique mahogany-cased clock on the wall ticked on and on, the time of departure came and went … I was already thinking about whether our plane had been filled with fuel yet. Had the pilot arrived with his cabin crew and flight attendants? Lisa, quite rightly, was saying goodbye to Alfie, doing what any mother would do if she was leaving her young son for a while, taking time to make sure everything was okay with him. I'll put my hands up to it: I was flapping.

Eventually she was ready. By now it was 2.10pm. Yes, that's all it was. I know you're going to think that ten minutes is no time at all, there should be nothing to worry about. What was all the fuss about? If you're the type of person that I am when it comes to timetables, it puts the first fear of being late in your mind. You're immediately thinking, 'How can we make this ten minutes up? Will we be all right?'

A wonderful film came out some years ago called *Clockwise*, starring John Cleese as a clock-watching headmaster who catches the wrong train, falls further and further behind schedule and becomes obsessed with getting to his destination. I'm not as bad as Cleese was in the movie, but let's just say I know where his character was coming from.

Josie was behind the wheel – quite fitting really, as she was the one who'd found the honeymoon destination – and off we went. The car crunched over the gravel drive, through the gate, headed south, onto the M25 … and into the most horrendous traffic jam you could imagine.

The M25 is a nightmare at the best of times: this was the worst of times. Nicknamed 'The Road to Hell', on the day we drove onto it, it was living up to the other nickname it has earned – 'The Biggest Car Park in the World'. One hundred and eighteen miles long in total, and I wouldn't have been surprised if it said on the radio that the entire length of it was gridlocked. I felt that it was going to be rock-solid all the way from Essex to Gatwick, a little matter of 60-odd miles.

So there we sat. We tried to be cheerful, we told each other it would clear up soon. And we sat and sat – and sat. I could see other drivers yawning and fiddling with their radios. Some were busy in conversation on their mobile phones, others trying to keep their fidgeting children amused in the back seats of people-carriers. We all had one thing in common: none of us were moving. To get the car in first gear was an achievement; to build up enough speed to have to change in second remained just a remote ambition.

It wasn't as though we were going over to Spain or France on a budget airline where, if we missed the plane, there would be another one along later in the day. The worst scenario would be catching one the next morning. This wasn't that sort of flight; we *had* to be there on time.

I managed to control my desire to say, 'I knew we should have left earlier.' The last thing I wanted to do was to be seen to be rubbing it in. It wouldn't have earned me any Brownie points, it would only have made things even more unbearable.

The worst thing about traffic jams – apart from not moving, that is – is not knowing what caused them or when they are going to clear up. Could it be a terrible accident? In that case, a delay is nothing compared to the agony the victims might be suffering. I'm only human, though, and everyone thinks, 'Couldn't they have picked tomorrow to crash?' This may sound callous, but it's true.

Perhaps it was roadworks, given that they are always digging the damn thing up for one reason or another. If that was the case, why on earth can't the Department of Transport – or whoever it is who does these things – organise it a bit better so the cars that are on the road can at least move?

We tried all the local radio stations for traffic news but we were still none the wiser. It got so bad that we telephoned the airport to let them know we were in a traffic jam. What they could have done, I don't know. Get ready for late arrivals, I guess, but at least it was better than doing nothing. We felt we were making some effort to get over this crisis. I was sitting there thinking it would be a miracle if we reached the Dartford Bridge, let alone Gatwick Airport.

Then, miracle of miracles, we started to move. Slowly at first, then we picked up speed. We stopped sneaking those sly looks at our watches that we'd resorted to and off we went – Gatwick beckoned.

Despite my panics and fears we got there in time – naturally – and I was able to have that cup of foaming latte at my leisure in the airport's Club Lounge. We were travelling British Airways in the Club section of the plane, so what better way of relaxing than enjoying a coffee – and a proper drink or two – scanning the magazines they provide and having a calming cigarette? Before anyone says that smokers should be banned or shot or whatever, I have tried to give up on numerous occasions. Sometimes I've kept off them for a decent period of time too, but in the end I've always been drawn back to the deadly weed.

Anyway, when the announcement came to board we headed for the departure gate, all our worries seemingly behind us. Soon we would be up, up and away, heading for those white sandy beaches and cobalt-blue skies.

What I hadn't done, though, was stock up with cigarettes. We'd practically exhausted our supply in the Club Lounge, but I reckoned that as we were not allowed to smoke on the plane there would be no point in hunting for ciggies around Gatwick. And they sell cigarettes in Mauritius, don't they?

As we settled into our seats and stretched our legs we looked forward to our meals, the in-flight movie, perhaps a glass or two of champagne. We were holding hands, looking into each other's eyes and telling anyone who cared to listen that we were off to get married. Absolute bliss.

Twelve-and-a-half hours later we landed and were both – as they say – dying for a fag. We were desperate. You could probably say we were beyond desperate. That's when the trouble started.

We'd come off a plane where smoking was banned, across tarmac where you couldn't light up and into a luggage hall where it was forbidden too. Of course, there was nowhere to buy cigarettes in a baggage reclaim hall anyway, and even if there had been then it would have been no good as I didn't have any local currency on me.

But we did have one cigarette left. Yes, just the one, and it was nestling all on its own in my golden Benson & Hedges packet, which had been in my pocket for over half a day. If I'd had two cigarettes, no problem, we could have had one each. If I'd had none, then at least we would be in the same agonising position as each other. But I had just the one. And that's why it kicked off.

I decided to go to the toilet for a wee and while I was in there light up the cigarette. Lisa had a different take on the situation. She said, 'Give it to me, I'll have half and you can finish it when you come back.'

I said, 'No, you can wait. I'll have half and then when I come out I'll give it to you and you can finish it off.' A bit of a Mexican stand-off was developing.

Lisa came back, quick as a flash: 'No, give it to me. You're going for a wee and you can't have a wee and a cigarette at the same time.' There is, it must be said, a certain irrefutable logic in that statement. Don't think about it too long, though, as it doesn't conjure up too pretty an image.

By now I'd lost it. 'Here you are, if you're so desperate!' I shouted, and threw it at her.

Lisa – my darling Lisa, whom I love like life itself and who'd flown with me halfway around the world on this joyous expedition – then came back with the type of phrase you don't normally hear from a bride-to-be: 'Stick it up your arse then!'

There we were, at the start of the holiday of a lifetime, surrounded by all these middle-aged, middle-class Brits also on their dream vacation, who were waiting for the luggage to clatter into life on the carousel. It was probably one of the ugliest scenes they'd had in the Sir Seewoosagur Ramgoolam International Airport – try saying that after a drop of bubbly – for quite some time.

I brought this particular episode to an end by picking the cigarette up and taking it into the toilet. I lit up and smoked it all from delightful first draw to last satisfying drag. Then I walked out to meet up with Lisa again. She didn't get near that last ciggie of mine and, if you'll excuse the pun, she was blazing mad over it.

Looking back, I'll hold my hands up to the fact that my behaviour wasn't what you'd call top-drawer during this particular episode. Not the best of starts, then. And it was about to get worse.

15

The Hotel from Heaven

I was fuming. There I was, standing at the international airport in Mauritius having had a good old-fashioned slanging match with my bride-to-be over a cigarette. I was mad; she was madder. We weren't really talking. Just to make matters worse, there was no sign of my helicopter.

Yes, I did say helicopter.

It hadn't been all that long ago that I'd been going to Millets to get a tent for a weekend's camping holiday in Hastings and been quite excited over the prospect. Now here I was on an idyllic Indian Ocean island irate that my chopper hadn't turned up. What was the world coming to? No sign of the pilot, no sign of the machine, no sign of anything ...

That, you see, was part of the luxury package I'd arranged. We were due to be whisked in a helicopter from the airport straight to the hotel. We would arrive in style on the hotel landing pad, climb out elegantly and, ducking slightly to avoid the downdraft, be in our room in moments. That was the plan, anyway. I'd spent all this money on the holiday and it was going pear-shaped at a great rate of knots.

Eventually a little man appeared and identified himself as being from the hotel. There had been a mix-up, confusion, call it what you will, but we didn't have a helicopter to greet us – there wasn't one spare, we'd have to go by car.

The driver gave us a great, big friendly smile and said, 'Welcome to Mauritius.' If looks could kill he'd have been dead on the spot. Lisa and I still weren't talking and you could cut the tension with a knife as we climbed into the car. The driver looked at us in his rear-view mirror and obviously thought he'd come out with some friendly banter but, detecting the mood, he stayed quiet. A wise move on his part. He was probably thinking, 'These English are a funny lot' or, 'Their marriage won't last.' He might have been right on the first point, but he was way off target with the second.

The car glided away from the airport terminal. I looked out of my rear-side window, Lisa looked out of hers. If we'd gone to Norway the atmosphere couldn't have been any icier.

We looked out at the scenery on that hour-long drive to the hotel. We may have spoken, I can't remember for sure, but I don't think we did. If we did, it must have been in words of one syllable. We certainly didn't have anything approaching a conversation. Not the sort of behaviour you would expect to see from the bride- and groom-to-be in the run-up to the greatest day of their lives.

The countryside was beautiful: bougainvillea and

anthodium jostled for space, the pomegranate and mango trees groaned under the weight of their fruit and the yellow flowers of the Indian laburnum moved in the light wind. We looked at the shanty towns along the roadside and detected the smells of the small bars and food stalls selling cheap curries, a host of other spicy meals, an endless variety of fish dishes and the local speciality of pancakes served with a hot bean curry and a dollop of tomato chutney.

We could have been back in Epping High Street for all the difference it made.

By the time we had got to the hotel things hadn't got any worse, mercifully, but they certainly hadn't improved.

Every guest at the hotel is 'gonged in' when they arrive for the first time, a Mauritian custom involving one of the staff banging a little gong to greet you. Then the manager came to meet us. All very nice, charming and polite, but we still weren't in a good mood. I could have mentioned the missing chopper, but I let it go. Looking back, it might have been fun to come out with the line, 'Where was my helicopter, my good man?' It wasn't the right time or place, though, and it wouldn't actually have been my style.

The manager said, 'Let me show you to your room' … and it turned out it wasn't the room we had requested. This was going from bad to worse. We pointed out that we had asked for a room on the ground floor so that we could just walk out and onto the beach. Instead we had been placed alongside the garden, on a different height. So we said we wanted a different room and the staff ran off to see what they could do.

In fairness to them, they couldn't have been more helpful. One of the female members of staff disappeared, reappeared and told us we were being moved.

Things could only get better, surely – and thankfully, pretty soon they did.

The porters picked up our baggage, loaded it on the trolley and moved us to the room of our dreams. As we looked around it I spoke to my butler. I think I've forgotten to mention that the hotel provides you with your own butler – here I was, Joe Johnson from Edmonton with his own Jeeves after all those years. I say 'mine' – actually I had to share him with Lisa. Still, that wasn't a problem. Nor was there much difficulty in deciding what his first task would be. 'Pop down and get us some cigarettes. Straightaway, please,' I asked him. Within moments he was back, Lisa and I were able to light up and that put us both in a calmer mood. We looked at each other and didn't really need to say anything, we were both thinking the same: 'Here we are in the lap of luxury in a beautiful country, about to get married and we're rowing over a stupid cigarette.'

The Cold War between us was thawing out at a great rate of knots. We sat on the bed and cuddled each other; then we really cuddled each other. I'm not going into more detail than that, but we both felt better afterwards.

If surroundings like this were new to me, they were even newer to Lisa. We'd been to a decent hotel in Tenerife to make up for our nightmare holiday, but she had never experienced opulence like this before. Neither had I.

After our 'cuddles', Lisa walked out onto the terrace and looked around her. The Indian Ocean was the kind of clear blue only poets can describe; the sand as white as a painting. The nearby lagoon seemed calmness itself. In the distance the sun was shining on the green sugarcane-clad mountains. No setting could be more perfect. Lisa took it all in slowly as if actually tasting the beauty of it all – and she started to cry.

But these weren't tears of anger or sadness; this was sheer joy. The foolishness of the last few hours was forgotten and she was so overwhelmed by happiness that the tears gushed out of her. She had always dreamt of being in a place like this and now she was. I was practically crying with her, it was all so wonderful.

This is as good a time as any to describe the hotel. I don't want to sound as though they've hired me to be their public relations officer, but it is breathtaking. We had one of their Ocean Suites, decorated in beige, earth and spice. It had a separate giant lounge, private dining room and two secluded terraces leading off the master bedroom. An al fresco shower meant you could rinse off outside after a dip in the sea and there was even a patio for us to relax outside on. The room, with its plush upholstered sofas, had giant bay windows complete with sliding shutters. The bathroom had a huge tub, big enough for two or more, as well as a walk-in shower. No matter how hot you ran the water, the mirrors stayed clear, thanks to their anti-steam surface. (No, I don't know how it works either.) Egyptian cotton sheets, so clean it was practically alarming, covered the king-size bed and the pile of pillows were stuffed with goose down. No wonder we were in seventh heaven.

If she wanted it, Lisa could go to the hotel spa with its eight treatment rooms and a vast range of services, including facial and body treatments, massages, hydrotherapy, sauna and herbal wraps. Or she could visit the hotel hairdresser. Come to think of it, so could I. And although we weren't there to keep fit, there was a superbly equipped gym – personal trainer provided, if wanted – and a golf course and tennis courts as well as a host of water sports such as windsurfing or deep-sea fishing.

I haven't even mentioned the grub yet. There were a host of places where we could eat and drink. The finest restaurant was the Spoon des Iles, with a range of dishes from literally all over the world, although you could dine in a room called Paul and Virginie, which specialised in fresh seafood and Mauritian goods. We developed a soft spot for La Terrasse, though, which surrounded the pool and overlooked the ocean. Marvellous. There were bars all over the place too, including the Golf Club Bar and the Casino Bar. You couldn't move for cocktails or fine wines; it was almost embarrassing to ask for a beer.

And if you went to the beach, you didn't have to go without there either. To get food or drink you'd simply wave a little flag the hotel had given you and one of the staff, who were continually walking along the sand, would scurry over and take your order.

We got our first, slightly uncomfortable, taste of this lifestyle within minutes. The chambermaid arrived and asked if Lisa wanted to have her bag unpacked and the clothes put away; Lisa declined and told her she'd do it herself. The reason for that was simple: she'd always unpacked her own bags and the very idea of someone grabbing hold of your clothes and then hanging them in a wardrobe was alien to her. She didn't want to see someone serving her in that way. It was no problem to the chambermaid, that's what she did for a living, but Lisa was ill at ease with the idea of being waited-on too much. She'd managed all these years, after all, so why change?

One thing mustn't be overlooked in all this: we still had a wedding to get through.

Just because you're thousands of miles from home in an idyllic setting, the planning doesn't stop. Sadly, it wasn't going to be a case of getting dressed one morning and popping down to the beach, standing under a canopy and back to the bar in twenty minutes' time. If only it had been that simple.

We had to sort out flowers, the videoing of the ceremony, the music, hairdressers – His and Hers – getting our clothes pressed again after the flight … After all the problems from the cigarette incident were finally resolved, that first day was spent on preliminary arrangements and making sure we were on top of things.

By the time evening came, we were starving. We went to the best restaurant in the hotel and who should we see there but footballer Eric Cantona. He made his name playing for

Manchester United and France and was renowned as a wonderful player, but he's probably best remembered in this country for leaping over the touchline wall at Crystal Palace's ground and launching a flying karate kick at a fan who had insulted him.

Fortunately, he was in a much more pleasant mood that night. He was with his wife, his brother and another man, and I thought I'd go and introduce myself. I explained that we were on holiday and planned to get married the next week. Then I thought I'd chance it, and asked him if he would be a witness, as we hadn't got anyone lined up for the role yet.

To my astonishment, he said he'd love to. This was going to be fun: one of soccer's fieriest characters doing the honours on the biggest day of my life. Lisa and I were, as they say in football, over the moon about it all. Then came the let-down. 'Which day next week did you say it was?' he asked, in that thick French accent of his. When we told him he said he was sorry, but that was the day he was checking out and had to hurry back to the airport for his flight home. He did seem genuinely apologetic that he couldn't make it. Ah well – so near and yet so far.

The food in the restaurant was out of this world. A superb bottle of wine would be waiting for you on your table, not that you had to drink it, and somehow or other every member of staff knew your name. They all knew us as 'Mr and Mrs Johnson'.

In a sense I felt the same way Lisa did when she wouldn't

let the chambermaid unpack her bags. It was quite humbling to be waited on hand and foot in this manner; I just wasn't used to it. I know it's their job and they get paid for it, but it was service the like of which I'd never come across before. If you decide to have the buffet you load up your plate and the second it's full a member of staff takes it out of your hand, walks alongside you back to your table and then places it down for you. At least we weren't the only ones who had their feathers ruffled by this. One woman piled her plate high and when the waiter came to take it out of her hands she refused to hand it over. She must have thought he was going to steal it!

I mentioned there was a lot of arranging to be done before the ceremony and that in turn proved to be hard work. All right, I know there aren't going to be too many tears shed for me in the position I was in, but it was hot and humid there and I just wanted to chill out by the pool. Instead, on one day we did nothing but administration linked to the ceremony.

We had to drive to the island capital, Port Louis, to see the town clerk over something or other. He was a charming chap, but a bit different from local government officials back home in that he wore a short-sleeved shirt and a rather natty pair of shorts.

Then it was off for what seemed like another 50-mile drive to meet the registrar. We had to take Lisa's divorce papers with us to prove she was no longer married. And then we encountered an aspect of Mauritian law that took our breath away.

Our wedding was conducted under their legal system and that states that if a woman is recently divorced, as Lisa was, then they have to make sure there are no disputes over the fatherhood of any baby she might have in the near future. In other words, that there can't be two possible 'legal' fathers to the child. How do they get round this? The bride-to-be has to have a pregnancy test, that's how!

I kid you not, Lisa had to go to a clinic, with me tagging along, and do a wee-wee for them. Talk about embarrassing! She knew she wasn't pregnant, but that wasn't good enough for them. So we had to sit for about four hours at this clinic while her sample was being tested. All the time we could see the sunlight outside and we thought of long cocktails in tall, thin glasses by that Olympic-size pool back at the hotel. In our dreams … in our dreams.

16

Two Perfect Weeks

Our wedding day – 8 October 2001 – dawned and it was as beautiful and sun-filled a day as you could wish for. After the heartache and struggles I'd suffered over the years, it was hard to take it all in. It wasn't just me either. Remember, Lisa had been working in Panini's just a few months earlier and now she was here, on this staggeringly gorgeous island, helicopters at the ready, surrounded by luxury and hob-nobbing with people like Eric Cantona. Whenever she thinks of that day she utters just one word: 'Unbelievable'.

The day itself went so smoothly it exceeded even our greatest expectations. First of all we popped into the jewellers in the hotel and got Lisa a necklace and earrings for around £3,000. Why not? I know she didn't need them, she had enough jewellery for the ceremony, but I'd been giving the shop the once-over every time I passed by and I thought it would be ideal to get that last-minute gift before the wedding.

Then it was back to our suite so the hotel hairdresser could titivate Lisa's hair, and mine too, come to that. Once we had been spruced up we got into our best wedding gear – the stuff that with the help of Josie we had sweated blood to choose in London – ready for the show. All of a sudden we heard this 'boom, boom, boom' as a band struck up outside the suite in the grounds nearby. It was the local Sega band, playing just for us. As we came out onto the beach they formed a circle around us and began dancing and singing; half-a-dozen beautiful dark-skinned girls dancing easily and naturally to the beat of the men playing the handheld drums and large tambourine-like instruments alongside them. All of them wore traditional colourful Mauritian costumes and they were our escort to the beachside wedding.

For those of you who don't know what Sega music is – and I don't blame you for that – it's the age-old dance music of Mauritius and some of the other Indian Ocean islands. It used to be played on some very basic percussion tools and a one-stringed guitar, but now modern instruments are used. The dance itself is a gentle, and sometimes not-so-gentle, movement of the hips to a pulsating rhythm that starts off with a sway and rises to a crescendo as the tempo of the music increases. It can be very sexy indeed, but that morning our minds were on other matters.

So off we started along the path through the lush green gardens with their black-and-white swans gently guarding a bevy of tiny, fluffy cygnets and headed to the beach. All around us people were lying on sun-beds near the pool by the sand, lapping up the lunchtime sunshine. There we were in our finery making our way between them and they all turned to have a look at the happy couple. You can't blame them with all the singing, dancing and music that was going on. I pity anyone who was trying to have a snooze out there that day before heading in for lunch – they had no chance.

At the beach there is this wonderful tradition of choosing a palm tree near the site of the wedding ceremony to carve your names on. We'd been down to the beach prior to the day itself and chosen a spot past the hotel helipad and near the shoreline for the actual ceremony. In between then and the big day, our names had been carved on a palm tree alongside the spot where the wedding was to happen. There they were for all to see: 'Joe and Lisa'.

The ceremony was hilarious in many ways. It was moving and romantic too, but it certainly had its funny moments. Every other word was 'love' or, to be more accurate, 'lurve'. The small official in his rather-too-large dark suit who was carrying out the ceremony spoke with the local Mauritian dialect, sounding slightly French to most British ears. It was all, 'Do you promise to lurve this man ...?' and, 'Do you promise to lurve this woman ...?' He must have said the word 'lurve' a hundred times.

Then came a real shocker. The registrar asked me, 'Do you promise to give her all of your wealth, some of your wealth or none of your wealth?' Talk about being put on the spot! I wasn't expecting that, I had no idea it was coming ... I hadn't gone through every word of the ceremony beforehand – who would? Perhaps he'd heard I'd won the Lottery, I don't know, but I was in no position to argue. I said, 'All of it.'

That wasn't the only thing that took me aback during the ceremony. As I've mentioned, the weather was hot and it had caused Lisa's wedding finger to swell up in the heat. We had a wedding ring each and they were placed on a tray for us in their smart Cartier box. I took Lisa's ring out and, lo and behold, it wouldn't go on the wedding finger on her left hand! I tried pushing it, winding it, twisting it, without success. I didn't want to use too much force, as I might have hurt her finger – and that wouldn't have been a very good start to married life.

It wasn't the first time we'd had trouble fitting it, either. We'd gone into Cartier in London about a month before the trip and asked to see a selection of wedding rings. Since the company was founded, in 1847, I don't think a couple so much in love as we were could have walked through its doors. As it's Cartier, they don't ask questions such as 'What price range, sir?' because that would be too obvious, unless you decide to ask them first. Instead, the staff – we were on first-name terms with them by then – bring you a selection and you choose the one you want. Then they tell you the price.

We wanted to buy two rings, one for each of us – His 'N' Hers rings, I suppose – and of course we chose Lisa's first. Together we selected a beautiful platinum ring with nine 22-carat diamonds set in it. It cost more than £10,000 … and it didn't fit! Cartier said it wasn't a problem and that they would send it to their Paris workshop to be altered, but we

The £100,000 party we threw to celebrate our wedding with all of our friends and family.

Above: Lisa, her sister Josie (*left*), friend Liz (*centre*) and me.

Below left: Lisa and my son Zak.

Below right: What a mover!

Our wedding.

Above: With Eric Cantona at the One & Only le Saint Géran Hotel in Mauritius.

Below: On the beach with the Sega dancers following the wedding ceremony.

After declaring our 'luurve' for one another, we lapped up the beautiful Mauritian surroundings and had an incredible four-course dinner.

Mille-feuille de coeur de palmier au marlin fumé
Heart of palm mille-feuille with smoked marlin

* * *

Bisque de langouste à l'armagnac
Crayfish bisque with armagnac

* * *

Assiette de fruits de mer grillés
Grilled mixed seafood platter

* * *

Crème brûlée de pistache verte avec sa glaçe aux noix de pécan caramelisé
Pistachio crème brûlée and its caramelised pecan nut ice-cream

* * *

Café ou thé
**Coffee or tea
Petits fours**

Above left: Me, Lisa and Alfie on board the Pride of Bilbao – off to Spain and new a life.

Above right: Alfie enjoying life in Puerto Banus. Going fishing …

Below left: … and playing in our pool.

Below right: Alfie and our gorgeous baby Blue.

Life in Spain.

Above: Lisa and the other Marbella Belles. © *Solarpix.com*

Below: Me, Lisa and our friends Francine and Adam in Bar Casar, Benahavis.

Lisa's fortieth birthday party.

Above: (*From left*): Flynn (my brother in law), Josie (my sister in law), Flynn (my nephew), Lisa, me and Alfie.

Below: (*clockwise from back left*): Our friend Gypsy Kathy, Lisa, friend Janet, friend Liz and Lisa's sister Josie.

Above left: Showing brother Danny Gibraltar

Above right: My kids Tina and Nick.

Below: Lisa and her friend Michelle.

Me with Lisa, Blue and Alfie at our home in Spain.   © *Solarpix.com*

were worried about running out of time as the wedding was getting near, so they arranged for it to go to their branch within Harrods.

What hadn't been taken into account was that it might not fit onto Lisa's finger if it swelled ever-so slightly in the sultry heat of the Tropics – but you can't think of everything, can you? At least Lisa saw the funny side of it and managed to smile before one of the witnesses of the ceremony came forward and helped slide it along her finger. Between the two of them they managed to push the ring into its rightful place and although it hurt her a little bit it was worth all the effort. We even laughed at the dilemma. Despite this mini-drama, Lisa looked stunning.

At least mine went onto my finger all right. It was less, how shall I put it, costly than Lisa's. Quite right too: the groom shouldn't outshine the bride. My ring – they called it a 'Love Ring' at Cartier – was white gold with six smaller diamonds running around it and a larger one in the middle. The cost? A 'mere' £5,000. Lisa subsequently had to take hers off once, when she had surgery, but apart from that we have not removed them to this day.

As expensive as the rings were, and as beautiful as Lisa looked, one of the most moving moments came when one of the two girl witnesses provided by the hotel read out a handwritten message from Lisa's sister Josie. She had faxed it through from England and was insistent that someone must read it out at the ceremony. I call it a 'message', but it was much, much more than that: it perfectly summed up both of our feelings on that fantastic day. It's worth repeating word for word. This is how it read:

As you embark on this new journey of marriage, think of it as a steady climb upon a steep and rocky hill.

Hold out your hand along the way and offer support when the path is winding.

Carry the load when the other tires and savour every moment of your time together when the going is easy. Obstacles will sometimes block your way, so look back at the tracks you have already made and move forward together. If you should reach a crossroad and cannot agree on the route ahead, be prepared to compromise.

Who knows which sex makes the better navigator?

If your feet are tempted to falter – rest, talk it through and draw strength from each other.

And finally, as you climb higher, the view below will be clearer and the hard work on the way to the top will be repaid in everlasting love.

Love Josie XXXXX

As we agreed to be man and wife, the Sega band started up again and the dancers began to do their thing. We had to join in, that was part of the ceremony. However, there was a slight problem – we had had a glass or two of champagne beforehand and, although we were far from legless, in that midday heat it all started to get on top of us. But we didn't let that stop us giving it all a go. I even tried my hand at serenading Lisa – first, with Nat King Cole's 'Unforgettable' and then Engelbert Humperdinck's 'Please Release Me'.

A video was made of us and I made a little speech along the lines of, 'This is the happiest time of my life. There's someone up there watching over us.' Then off we set back to the hotel through the lush gardens filled with lakes and exotic birds. The band was still playing behind us as we walked over the tiny 'Little Bo Peep' hump-back bridge in the grounds.

We climbed into a beautiful pink-and-white carriage, with 'Just Married' on the back, drawn by a single white pony that carried us on our way. All the time the band were playing their joyous music and there was a Sega dancer at the front of the horse banging away on his tambourine and singing. Then we went off round the nearby village and all the local people – and I'm not talking about tourists – were clapping and waving to us. This lasted about thirty minutes, then we went back to the hotel.

I know what you're thinking, that like all newlyweds we'd be heading straight for bed, perhaps to make 'lurve'. You're right in that we went straight to bed, but only to sleep – we were both so tired we just collapsed on the bed and crashed out!

It's a good job we did, as no sooner did we wake up than the wedding day turned into wedding night. We washed and got dressed in our finery again and prepared to head for our evening meal. All the time we were being videoed, as part of the presentation the hotel had for us, and we talked to the camera, explaining exactly what was going on and why, mainly for the benefit of our families who would one day be watching it. It was all so emotional that Lisa cried another small tear and no one could blame her.

We walked to the finest restaurant in the hotel with its marvellous French cuisine and there on the table was an embossed menu that read: 'Congratulations to Mr and Mrs Johnson. Saint Géran team wishes you Bon Appetit and everlasting happiness. Menu created by Chef Mesh and his brigade, 8 October 2001.'

And what a meal it was. The menu was in French, with an English translation in case our French was a leetle bit rusty, and it read like this:

Mille-feuille de coeur de palmier au marlin fumé
(Heart of palm mille-feuille with smoked marlin)

Bisque de langouste à l'armagnac
(Crayfish bisque with armagnac)

Assiette de fruits de mer grillés
(Grilled mixed seafood platter)

Crème brûlée de pistache verte avec sa glaçe aux noix de pécan caramelisé
(Pistachio crème brûlée and its caramelised pecan nut ice-cream)

To round it all off, we had the choice of coffee or herbal teas and a few petits fours to nibble on.

I told them I didn't want any of it, I'd prefer to have sausage, mash and onions. No, that's a joke, I was more than happy with the meal provided!

I looked at the table groaning under the weight of all that food, and the chilled champagne glasses in front of us, and I couldn't help but reflect that it was less than three years earlier that I had been driven to despair by my life. I had felt I was going nowhere and I didn't have the wherewithal to do anything about it. The nearest I got to champagne was walking past a bottle of it in an off-licence window. Now it was my tipple of choice with Lisa – Cristal, preferably.

Lisa must have noticed I was reflecting on the craziness of it all. I'd been through two marriage ceremonies before, one in a church and one in a registry office, but nothing like this. Surely similar thoughts were going through her head too, as she can't have dreamed a few months earlier of her life taking such a dramatic turn? At least I'd had over three years to get used to it all – for Lisa it must have been like being picked up by a hurricane and carried along by its force. It was only a year since we had met and a matter of months since she had been told of my wealth.

We walked across the bar area, although it felt as though we were gliding on air if truth be told, to where the music was playing and we were asked if there was a request that we would like to have played. There was – we asked for Eric Clapton's beautiful ballad 'Wonderful Tonight' and we danced to it in all our wedding finery. Clapton wrote it for his bride-to-be Patti – the idea came to him as he waited for her to get dressed to go out one night. It had always been one of my favourite songs and now I was with Lisa I understood even more completely the depth of feeling in the lyrics. I guess it's true that couples in love have a favourite tune or melody; well, there was no doubt that this song was now 'our song'. To this day the music still brings us together and reminds us of all the good times and the sheer pleasure of being in each other's company.

The five or six days that remained of our holiday passed in a haze of pleasure.

As we'd done on that very different break in Tenerife, we even 'escaped' one night to the beach and made love – we like to do that on holiday – with the sand between our toes and the moonlit sky above our heads. In the background we would hear the waves crashing on the shore and the sound of the energetic crickets in the hotel grounds. Our suite was so near the sea that I even dared Lisa to run down to the beach and back again in the nude – and she did it! And of course, if she did it, I had to do it too! We followed it with a quick bit of skinny-dipping and then back to the hotel. Nothing wrong with it, no one there to be shocked, just great honeymoon fun.

I'm not one to boast, or to go into too much detail, but when it came to lovemaking I was like a little bunny rabbit while we were there. In between our romantic activities we managed to fit in some paragliding and an undersea walk, before climbing on board the helicopter that was to take us back to the airport.

We agreed afterwards that it had been the two greatest weeks of our lives. I'd no idea if I was living above my means during this time; I wasn't bothered either. In the early days of my win, no matter how much I spent it seemed to be less than the interest the £10 million was earning me. It sounds very irresponsible, I know, but I didn't care. I simply knew that after a lifetime of struggle I was in seventh heaven.

The cost of the honeymoon, wedding and gifts? I haven't mentioned that yet, have I? It was £70,000 – and worth every single last penny!

17

Puerto Banus

Once we returned home there was some serious shopping to be done. I got Lisa a lovely Cartier watch for around £10,000 and also a silver Audi TT for £35,000, complete with a power convertible hood, black leather interior and roll bars; the works. It even had on its registration plate, by sheer coincidence, the letters OTT. The only trouble was, it was a two-seater and there were three of us if we wanted to take Alfie. So, after three or four months, we changed Lisa's car and got her a silver Mercedes Convertible CLK to replace the OTT Audi TT!

There were other changes in our lives too. We never used the flat in Docklands, so we sold it. In all the time that I owned the penthouse at Baltic Quays I can't remember using the oven even once. I don't think I used the washing machine either. You couldn't really say, by any stretch of the imagination, that I got full use or full enjoyment out of the place. Buying it had seemed a good idea at the time, although I guess I could have done better if I'd looked around a little bit more. I got what I paid for it, but given the amount I'd spent doing it up, including that spiral staircase for over £20,000, it wasn't the best of deals on my part. In real terms I made a loss, but I was never tempted to hang onto it.

As Lisa had moved in with me to Blackhall, we decided to look around the Essex area for somewhere that we could move into as a couple, a home that both of us had chosen. So we started looking around for larger properties nearby – lovely though it was, Blackhall only had three bedrooms. We found several places that we liked, but none of them quite filled the bill.

For New Year's Eve 2001 we decided to see the old year out in style. Lisa, myself, her sister Josie and her husband all went to Langan's Brasserie – which, as I've mentioned before, had become one of my favourite haunts. One of the things I've always liked about it is that there is no class distinction in there, which is how I think one of the founders of the place – the actor Michael Caine – wanted it. They had a set menu for New Year's Eve, although normally we stuck to our favourites – bangers and mash or liver and bacon: great English food cooked to perfection. The bill for the four of us that night managed to come in at £1,150, though, which meant it wasn't cheap. No, not because it was the most expensive plate of sausages in the history of the world … because we had several bottles of the best Dom Pérignon champagne that money could buy to wash it all down. It was

a marvellous night and we even had a star sitting near us –
David Soul of *Starsky and Hutch* fame.

We were living at Blackhall again and for the first time I
could quit the games and go to the village pubs with Lisa to
enjoy a drink and some food. At last, I could have a chat and
a beer without looking at my watch to make sure I was back
home before she returned and caught me out.

Around this time, we also discussed the possibility of Lisa's
parents moving into the annexe next door to the main house.
It was my idea – some men might have nightmares about
having the in-laws a few feet away from them; I'd always got
on very well with mine, though, and it seemed to me to be the
obvious thing to do. We put the idea to them and they agreed;
we made it cosy and comfortable and they moved in after
Christmas of 2001.

During this period we began to think of buying a property in
Spain. Josie and her husband had an apartment in the
Alcazaba complex at Puerto Banus and Lisa knew the area.
So we decided to look for somewhere there, purely as a
holiday home. Within a short time, we had found a two-
bedroom apartment for £255,000 and put five per cent down
straightaway, as you do in Spain.

I had always wanted to live in Spain. I'd been to the
mainland only once before when, after I'd won the Lottery,
someone recommended the Kempinski hotel nearby to me. I
had never been down to Puerto Banus, but as soon as I saw it
I fell in love with the place. I had visions of walking the dog

along the beach and going to the shops, which are right on top of you there.

For those of you don't know Puerto Banus, it's just a short drive from Malaga airport and only a few minutes from Marbella. It was built by the property developer José Banus – hence its name – and when it opened in 1970 among the glittering A-list celebrities there were the Aga Khan, *Playboy* founder Hugh Hefner, film director Roman Polanski and Prince Rainier of Monaco and his wife Princess Grace. Since then, the port has been synonymous with the rich, the famous and the beautiful. It has all the well-known brand-name shops you would expect to find in London, Paris or Rome, as well as moorings for 915 luxury yachts – one extravagance I haven't gone in for yet. I'm no party animal, but the nightlife around the marina is also renowned. Although it wasn't there at the time we bought, near to our apartment in the middle of a traffic island is a three-ton rhinoceros created by the eccentric Spanish artist Salvador Dalí. If anyone comes to see us it's always a good landmark for directions – after all, there aren't too many gigantic steel rhinos around!

Lisa and I had once been away for a break and left her parents looking after the house. When we got back, her mother gave us a note that someone had pushed through the letterbox. It read, 'If you ever decide to sell, please give us first refusal.' We kept it safe – and it was to come in handy. When we finally contacted the man who had said he'd buy Blackhall, he gave us £750,000 for it, plus money for the furniture. I'd made a good profit on the place although, in a way, I'd have loved to have kept it on. But we were impulsive in those days and we didn't give too much thought to the buying and selling of homes. It gave us the chance to buy a second apartment in the Alcazaba, though, and that's exactly what we did.

I was able to store the furniture from Blackhall that I hadn't sold at Tilegate Farm. We had all the furniture from the Docklands flat – good modern stuff that would be ideal for our new home in Spain – and we would be moving it from one contemporary apartment to another. I could easily have got a firm like Pickfords to move everything across, but, being an adventurous sort of chap, I decided to hire a van and do it myself.

We turned up at the Docklands with Zak and a couple of his gay friends. For some reason, following the renovations to the flat, the sofa that we had got into the place could no longer come out through the door. So we came up with a scheme whereby we'd lower it on a rope from the terrace – not all the way down, but just from the penthouse down to the next level – and from there we'd be able to move it.

Not being professional removal guys, we made hard work of it – at one stage I was holding onto the ropes myself, without any help, in order to prevent it plunging 12 or 13 floors to the ground! Eventually we got it down, with a little bit of damage, and then into the van.

We didn't have a big van, but you could spot it miles away. It was a company local to our home in Essex and the vehicle itself was called 'Supervan'. Unsurprisingly, it had a giant logo on the sides similar to the one that Superman has on his chest. Talk about keeping a low profile – not!

We were well overloaded, above and beyond the recommended weight maximum, but we were still incredibly excited when we arrived on the south coast to catch our ferry. Nothing could take the gloss off the excitement we were feeling. Well, that's what we thought, anyway …

The trip started to go wrong as soon as we saw our accommodation. We'd asked for a deluxe cabin with a separate bed for Alfie, but we ended up with something you couldn't swing the smallest cat in the world around in; Alfie's bed turned out to be something you pulled out from below one of the small bunks. Things got worse when we hit the Bay of Biscay. Talk about up and down, up and down – we thought it would never stop! It might have been the middle of summer, but someone had forgotten to tell the weather gods that, and it was dire. Our mood wasn't helped by the warnings we received about robbers in Spain. Apparently, they tap a nail into your tyre at a petrol station, follow you along the road until you stop with a flat tyre and then jump out and rob you. Charming!

The atmosphere on board was almost like a booze-cruise, so Lisa and I had a few drinks to help us survive. When we woke up the next morning we could see the Spanish shoreline in the distance and the port of Bilbao getting nearer by the minute.

We faced more problems when we arrived. I was going to drive and Lisa was to navigate, but we got confused by the road signs. They are all different in Spain from the UK ones and they have two signs at every junction – one for the toll motorway and one for the normal roads. That meant that every time we saw a sign we had a decision to make as to which one to follow!

After four or five hours of this, we saw a sign for Madrid. Hooray, we're on the right road! I was as happy as a sand boy. After we hit Madrid, though, we had to go around a very difficult mountain range; I could feel the van swaying as we went around every corner. It was obvious we had too much in it to be safe, but there was nothing we could do now, there was no going back. We even had a flat tyre to cope with, to add to our worries.

Fortunately, the mountain range and the flat tyre were all overcome and we were able to drive on. Soon we came upon a sign for Granada, so we knew we were closer to our destination. We were getting tired and ratty with every sign that we reached and then we saw one for Malaga. Joy of joys, that cheered us up and we thought we'd be there in an hour. It was nearer three or four hours, though, by the time we finally arrived.

The drive wasn't helped by the fact that we didn't have a useful word of Spanish between us. Café con leche (coffee with milk) was about as far as we got – that and being able to ask for the bill. We'd stop at a *hostal*, the low-priced Spanish hotels, for a bite to eat and the floor would be covered in cigarette butt-ends, paper serviettes and left-over food. Whenever we walked into one of them it was like a scene from a movie about the Wild West where all eyes turn round to see the strangers entering the saloon. We'd no idea what food to order, we'd just look at the tapas – the selection of dishes along the bar – and point. Lisa didn't eat a thing, though.

Eventually we got to Marbella and phoned up Lisa's sister, who was already in Spain, so was there to greet us. I'd driven the whole journey in one go and must have been behind the wheel for about 13 hours. Josie had a Chinese meal ready for us and no Chinese food has ever been so welcome as that meal was that night.

Our new life didn't get off to the best of starts, though, because no sooner had we arrived than one of the neighbours – a bit of a prat, if you ask me – said he didn't think I should leave the Supervan parked where it was, in my allotted parking space, because he thought it undermined the community – lowered the tone, if you like. I didn't take a blind bit of notice of him. Why should I? The van was there for a purpose. I was entitled to park it. End of conversation.

I'd love to be able to say that the first week in beautiful Puerto Banus went without a hitch. Being us, however, it didn't. Lisa and I had an argument.

I had to bring the van back to the UK and Lisa didn't want to come back with me. She'd hated the drive and wanted to travel home on the plane. I didn't want to drive all that way by myself, though. The row went on and on and it got worse as the week progressed. The van was due back on the Saturday, but we were never going to make it in time. I decided to keep it for another week and hope that Lisa would change her mind, but she wouldn't. We eventually made it up, but she was adamant she wouldn't come back with me, so I had to telephone Tina, who flew out to drive back with me. I could have afforded to keep it for another week, but by then I just wanted to get shot of it. What a fiasco!

People said to me, 'With all your money, why didn't you just have all the furniture shipped over?' and they had a point. But the truth was, I just liked the adventure of it all; I actually liked doing it a different way.

Soon after that we came over for another holiday, and that's when I approached Lisa and said, 'Lise, how do you fancy living here?' At first, she told me, 'I don't know.' Much to my surprise, however, almost immediately she added, 'But let me think about it.' I asked her again in a couple of hours and she said, 'Come on, let's go for it!' She said that if she didn't like it in a year we would come back, and that was obviously fine too.

Over time, we were to find that whenever we came back to England from Spain – although it was great to see our families – we found ourselves thinking, 'What am I doing here?' We both just wanted to be back in Spain. I guess when you make a move like that you are going to fall into one of two camps: either 'Why did we ever leave home and come here?' or, 'Let's get back to Spain as quickly as possible!' We definitely fell into the second category.

The sale of Blackhall went through so quickly that Lisa and I had to move into a hotel for the final month we were in England as the new buyer wanted to move in immediately and we couldn't keep him waiting. As we'd sold him virtually all the furniture at Blackhall too, apart from the stuff we stored at Tilegate, we only had the clothes we stood up in – but there were quite a lot of them! I only had the Range Rover at this stage so I hired a trailer to tow along behind me so we could take all our gear for Spain. The only problem was that although I was all right at reversing the large van, I was no good at all at reversing with a trailer; I couldn't do it to save my life.

Lisa didn't want to come with me as she'd had enough of driving through Spain the first time round, so I asked my brother Charlie to come with me. He wasn't going to do any of the driving, as he was well into his seventies by this stage. It was just to keep me company.

This time the crossing went smoothly. We decided to go Southampton-Cherbourg and then drive through France. We drove across the border and stopped the night at a small motel near Bilbao. We ate a meal there, although I could hardly keep my eyes open as I was so tired, and then we went to bed. There were two double beds in the room and I collapsed on one while Charlie went to sleep in the other. I thought that nothing on earth would keep me awake as I was so tired – but I was wrong. Charlie started to snore. Not just a normal sort of snoring, but the kind of noise on par with an air-raid warning siren in the war, and he kept it up all night – it was almost superhuman the way his breathing passages could create this wall of sound. By the time he woke up and we started to get ready for the next day's drive, I was even more exhausted than when I went to bed the previous evening!

On we went and yet again I had to get around Madrid, and this time there was the added complication of having the trailer to tow. We hadn't had to stop too much, as the Range Rover didn't use too much diesel, but eventually, near the Spanish capital, we had to stop to fill up. Then, horror of horrors, a car pulled in front of me on the station forecourt. The driver disappeared somewhere and that meant I'd have to reverse in order to get out. This would be the first time that I'd had to reverse the trailer and I wasn't looking forward to it one little bit.

I heard a scraping sound, whether it was a parked car or the petrol pumps I don't know, but I decided there was only one thing to do: unhook the trailer, pull it away by hand, then drive in front of it and reconnect the thing. The sun was beating down as myself and Charlie – who is well into his seventies, remember – started towing the trailer and everything in it to a more open part of the forecourt, where we were able to carry out the manoeuvre without causing any more damage to body, soul or motor vehicles.

We managed to make the rest of the journey without mishap and when we arrived at Puerto Banus we were greeted by Lisa, who'd flown down with Charlie's wife Maisie. Now, Maisie is wonderful, I love her to bits, but she does bear a striking resemblance to Bette Davies in *Whatever Happened to Baby Jane* with that over-the-top make-up. (Only joking Maisie!) Charlie and Maisie wanted to go to Gibraltar to have a look at the place and it's not a long drive from where we lived, so one day we set off to go there. All the time Maisie was back-seat driving – 'Joey, be careful this' and 'Joey, be careful that' – and when we started going over to Gibraltar, over the mountain, she would pipe up, 'Oh, be careful of the edge!' and 'Oh, watch out for the drop!' Eventually I had to stop the car and shouted at her, 'Shut up!'

After they had been with us a week, it was time to take them both back home. I decided to drive them back in one go, in 24 hours. It seemed a lot longer, as every time we stopped, Maisie, who moved around with the help of a Zimmer frame, would shuffle off to the toilet, or take her pills or whatever. When you have a long drive like that all you want to do is push on – it's only normal. I'd stop for fuel and after 15 or 20 minutes there'd be no sign of her. Eventually she would appear and say she couldn't find the toilet, so we'd have to start all that waiting again …

At about one or two in the morning they'd dozed off. When Charlie woke up I'd ask him if we should find somewhere to stop the night, but he was always happy to crack on. The Channel Tunnel was never so welcome as it was that time I reached it with Charlie and Maisie. What an experience! I vowed never to do that drive again – though of course I have …

We'd often come out on the balcony of our home in Puerto Banus and look at the beautiful surroundings – the lawns, plants, trees and giant swimming pool below – and have a cuddle and reflect on how lucky and happy we were.

But you've probably gathered by now that although Lisa and

214

I are crazy about each other we do have the odd disagreement now and again. Nothing unusual in that, all married couples disagree from time to time, but it led to an incident when I was far from happy about being on the balcony.

We had a row one night and I went over the top with a few of the things I said. We ended up arguing and Lisa got to the stage where she had simply had enough of me. I went out on the balcony, stark naked – and Lisa locked me out! It was the height of the season and the place was packed. We are above ground level, but only by one floor, and the grounds outside were teeming with people. I was pleading with her, 'Lisa, Lisa, let me in.' She didn't – instead, she kept me out there for four hours. I was in agony and as the evening wore on and became darker I started to get freezing cold. I was too embarrassed to call out for help and ask a stranger to fetch a ladder or come round to the apartment to try and rescue me. Of course, I had to pee at some stage and was forced to do it in the gully around the balcony. (I hope it didn't do too much damage to the potted plants in the vicinity and I certainly won't be making a habit of it.) Although we are not very high it still wasn't possible for me to climb down. And what would I have done then, anyway? Run around in the nude trying to get back in the front way?

Lisa just went to bed and left me, but – thankfully – she eventually relented and let me back in. When she did, we just smiled at each other and knew it was all over.

When we moved to Puerto Banus full-time we had a whole new bunch of neighbours to get on with. Some of the owners aren't here a lot or rent their places out, but some do live here all the year round. I like to think I'm fairly chatty and friendly and I would say to the people I met in Puerto Banus that if there was anything that they wanted doing or any favours then I would be there for them. I'd let people use my port pass, which means they can take their cars into the port – which is very helpful, believe you me – and I have equipment for starting cars, which also comes in handy if some people have left their vehicles for months on end without running them. I was asked if I would join the committee who help run the urbanisation, the development we lived in, and I found that quite flattering.

A typical day for us in Spain would begin with one of us dropping Alfie off at his school – and then the world would be our oyster. We might come back and go to the beach, which we love; have a drop of sangria; perhaps some paella … or, of course, we might go shopping in Puerto Banus. We might have to change the routine if we had to pick Alfie up from football training, but that was about it.

Then came the day that Lisa decided she wanted to do something in the way of business and I made a big, big mistake in encouraging her. It turned out that she wanted to make a venture into children's designer wear.

At the time, one of the girls, who was later to appear in the TV programme *Marbella Belles* alongside Lisa, had a shop in Puerto Banus called 'Posh'. The premises next door to it were vacant, so she suggested that Lisa should go into business there with a children's clothes shop and call it 'Angels at

Posh'. We knew there would be a market for this type of outlet, as a lot of the English couples in the area are more than happy to spend £200 or more on items like jeans for their kids.

So we rigged the shop out, at a lot of expense, with a sales counter, a bench, lighting decorations etc. and then we had to buy the stuff to sell. We went to several outlets in England, and several in Barcelona – and we bought loads of great children's designer stuff. It was a good day out for us. We'd fly from Malaga to Barcelona and buy really good stuff there – 'We'll have six of those and twelve of those!' The shop looked fantastic. We even stocked the Birkenstock range of shoes, which were very fashionable.

All our friends over here who had a bit of money would come to the shop, because they knew that it was good-quality stuff they were buying. We also had some useful advice from a friend who lived down here and owned a chain of shops in Birmingham.

The rent was 1,200 Euros a year, but we were buying stock left, right and centre … and I soon started to worry about the stock we weren't shifting. We were earning money – we even had a professionally-run fashion show for the kids' clothes in our apartment – but we never recovered the money we were putting into it. It was Lisa's project and I didn't enjoy it. I wasn't over the moon about the entire thing, but I did get involved in buying with her and putting things up in the shop.

Around this time we decided to go back to Mauritius for a holiday, just Lisa, myself and Alfie. There was one of those factory outlet shops near the hotel, close to a village, and we went to it as Lisa was thinking of buying some clothes for the shop. Part of the holiday involved going into these shops to look at the merchandise with a view to buying it for the store. (Personally, I thought this was a waste of time on what should have been a break, but there you go …)

One of them was run by an Indian man who was really on the ball. He asked us to come back to his office and told us we could select any designer label gear we wanted. He was running his business from his house, which had a big storeroom out the back, and we went there with him – although I did worry slightly that we might end up being kidnapped! But we weren't – quite the opposite, in fact – he went overboard and entertained us regally. After a while, he started showing us various items of clothing and we told him how much we liked them. It seemed like good gear to us … but then he turned round and said, 'Right, what label do you want putting on them?' We thought he was kosher, but the truth of the matter was that he was churning out the stuff and putting any 'designer' label on it that you wanted.

There was no way that we were going to go down that road. To begin with, it's not our style to pass cheap stuff off as expensive. And also, if we had bought some of his items and then it came to light in Puerto Banus that they were dodgy, our reputation would have been in tatters. The place is like a village in that respect. End of story.

18

Flights of Fancy

Quite a large portion of the population would reckon that living where we do – in the most glamorous part of the Costa Del Sol – life is one long holiday. What they'd be forgetting, though, is that if you are here for most of the year then you need to get away at times. I'm not saying that it becomes boring, simply that we need a break, in the same way everybody does.

We have a travel agent in Nueva Andalucia whom we use for all our exotic holidays. We book our flights back to the UK ourselves, but if it's somewhere special then, in the same way we used to go to our agent in Epping, we pop in to see the people near us in Spain and they fix everything up.

As well as our Mauritius breaks – we've been there three times since our honeymoon – we've been to the Maldives, Cyprus, Portugal, the Seychelles and Milan for shopping trips. We always stay in top-class hotels, usually five-star –

and why not? I know I've waxed lyrical about the beautiful beaches of Mauritius where we got married, but the white sands of the Maldives really are beyond description too.

We landed at the main airport at Male when we went there, but then it's four-and-a-half hours or so by boat to the island where we stayed. That was a bit too long for us, so we went by sea-plane instead. It could only take six passengers, but what a fantastic journey. Looking out of the 'chopper' you can see the shapes of the sharks and the stingrays in the clear water below. Magnificent!

We stayed in a water bungalow. Now, perhaps that conjures up images of a thatched roof with just a long table inside and a basic bed to rest on. Nothing could be further from the truth. Inside it is like a six-star hotel, if there is such a thing. Our bungalow had a king-size bed, a massive walk-in shower and the highlight of the building was a gigantic square of thick glass in the middle of the floor in the living area that you could look down through and see all the fish swimming around below. I know you can see tropical fish on television in Britain, but the snorkelling and diving around the bungalow made it all look like nothing in comparison. Alfie and I would snorkel every day; it was truly amazing.

There were gardens nearby and they were kept tidy by a team of about eight women who would come in on boats and tend them. We would go out of our way to chat to them and say how nice everything looked and they were amazed at that. It seems that most people – and if you go to the Maldives on holiday from Europe, the odds are that you are comparatively wealthy – just ignored them or took what they were doing for granted. I'm not that sort and never will be. A couple of them spoke good English, so we would have quite lengthy chats with them. Why other visitors don't do the same is beyond me, it really is.

While we were there it was Lisa's birthday, so I decided to hire a boat for the evening as a surprise treat. There were only myself, Lisa and Alfie on board, apart from the crew, of course. At one point, the captain said to me, 'Mr Johnson, what sort of music does your wife like?' Well, I wasn't too sure of her musical taste at this time so I just said, 'Elvis Presley' and left it at that. Off we went with the on-board chef in his white hat getting our meal ready and, as we sailed around the islands, all of a sudden the brilliant opening lines to the King's 'Blue Suede Shoes' start booming out across the quiet ocean waves.

I don't remember how much the boat hire cost, but it was well worth it. When we go on holiday we don't like to scrimp and save – we like to enjoy ourselves and the cost is secondary. The Maldives hold a special place in our memories. On one island the local people greeted us with King Coconut drinks – coconut milk and alcohol inside the shell. On another, on the beach, I wrote 'I Love You Lisa' in giant letters in the sand.

But of all the holidays we had – apart from our honeymoon – perhaps the craziest of all was the one to celebrate my sixtieth birthday. Now, when Lisa and I go on holiday, we invariably have three suitcases more than most people take with them. Well, when it came to packing for the big Six-O there was an added complication.

Lisa only told me that we were going back to the UK from Spain and I thought it would be for a boring 'surprise' party, which isn't my scene at all. What I couldn't figure out was why she was keeping me away from going into my wardrobe in Spain. For a week before we were due to depart for England she was almost patrolling the room to make sure I didn't start looking around for clothes.

The reason was simple: even though my birthday is in January, she was busy secretly packing away all my shorts, swimming gear and T-shirts. If I'd noticed they were missing, I'd have figured out pretty quickly that we wouldn't be heading for home. You don't have to be a genius to figure out that swimming shorts aren't a 'must' for Essex in the depths of winter …

We started off by flying from Malaga back to England. For the first three days that we were back in Essex, I was driving Lisa mental with my moaning. It didn't strike me as a particularly great way to spend my birthday. 'I don't want to be here,' I complained. 'It's cold, it's freezing. I don't want a party here!' I later found out that she told Josie that she didn't think she could keep up the pretence any longer; she had got a surprise in store for me and really wanted to let the cat out of the bag. The main reason for her wanting to do that was that I was becoming unbearable! But Josie calmed her down and said that although it was bad that I was walking around like a bear with a sore head at the moment, the real holiday treat would come as an even greater surprise to me.

We'd been back in England a few days and then, all of a sudden, four or five of our suitcases were all packed ready for the off. A taxi arrived at the door and pretty soon we were driving past Watford, so I realised that we were on the way to Heathrow. We'd already been out with the family for a big evening meal and I assumed that that had been the 60th-birthday bash, so I figured perhaps this was for a private helicopter lesson or something.

Of course, the luggage made me start thinking we were going somewhere a little further away, but I had no idea where.

We got in the check-in queue and Lisa told me that we were going on a shopping trip to Milan. All well and good – but it was a lie. I didn't bother to check the flight details on the airline counter because by this time I was used to simply handing my passport in, watching the luggage disappear behind the check-in guy or girl and then following Lisa, lemming-like, into the departure lounge.

Lisa got to the counter before I did and whispered something to the check-in girl. She was actually telling her that we were heading for Mauritius as she handed over our tickets, but she also whispered that it was a surprise and warned the girl not to let on our destination. Credit where it's due, the check-in girl didn't let it slip out. I was still in the dark.

We were flying Club Class, that much I knew, so we went straight in to the Club Lounge at Terminal 4. We were having a glass of champagne when there was an announcement over the loudspeaker that passengers heading for Mauritius should head for their gate to board. I didn't pay much attention to it – Lisa and Alfie didn't move, so why should I? They waited and waited, and after about ten or fifteen minutes they stood up and headed for the exit. As soon as you come out of the Club Lounge in that terminal you are opposite boarding Gate Number 2, and that was where the Mauritius flight was leaving from.

As we came past Gate 2 I looked at it and thought, 'Lucky devils, they are off to Mauritius!' Lisa walked past it, headed towards another gate … and then, all of a sudden, turned round and went back to Gate 2. Then the penny finally dropped. My flight to Milan was a thing of the past; it was going to be Mauritius again!

I know I go on about the island a lot, but if you've ever been there you will know why: it is pure magic. Add to that the memories that I have and it explains why Lisa and I will always have a special place in our hearts for the island. I sat in the Club compartment of the plane for the long flight and the tears started to roll down my cheeks, tears of pure joy at the thought of returning to that fantastic place.

When we finally landed it was like being with old friends. The staff of the hotel welcomed us as if we were part of their family – which, in a way, we had become.

On my birthday we had champagne and oysters on the beach. Nearby was Princess Caroline of Monaco and her family, who were also staying at the same hotel. I've mentioned them before and they were regulars at the hotel, so the place was full of paparazzi trying to take her photographs – unless it was me they were after, of course! She seemed very nice and, dare I say it, ordinary in the nicest sense, and during our stay she often had a friendly chat with us; Alfie swam in the ocean alongside her sometimes. Who would have thought that just a few years earlier, when I'd been penniless and looking forward to a couple of days in a cheap tent, that I'd be celebrating my 60th in the lap of luxury alongside royalty? So it was that on the evening of my birthday, 26 January, I took to the dance floor wearing the same ice-blue suit I'd worn on our wedding day and Lisa wore her wedding dress, albeit shortened so it could be worn at night; we danced to our song – Eric Clapton's 'Wonderful Tonight'. The famous lyric about makeup and long blonde hair always reminds me of my Lisa.

I've such happy memories of the island that I could go on forever about it. There was a beautiful waterfall inland and I remember diving off into the water beneath it. We went for beach barbecues with lobster and giant pink prawns, all washed down with rum. You could get half-cut in no time at all. Sometimes you could feed the fish with bread by hand, and the colours and shapes they came in are beyond description. I've got a permanent reminder of the holiday too – Lisa bought me an engraved Rolex Daytona for about £6,000 to celebrate my birthday.

Later, we went on a third holiday to Mauritius, and on that occasion we took Lisa's mum, Shirley, and her dad, Joe. They adored it in exactly the way that we did when we first visited the place. I'll never forget the look on their faces when we landed on the island and they saw how beautiful it was.

They were in the next room to us at the hotel and Shirley was looking out of the window at the birds in the gardens as she began to unpack. We had to tell her not to bother, as the staff did all that for you – shades of that first time Lisa and I went there.

We even went on an undersea walk with Shirley. She was in her late sixties by this time and she was scared of water, but she still decided to give it a go, despite all the gear and see-through helmet she had to wear. Sadly, Shirley has passed away since then, but she absolutely adored her submarine jaunt – it was one of the highlights of the holiday – and we are so glad that we were able to do that for her before she died.

I always got on well with Lisa's mum; we always used to be joking and laughing. I had a couple of good-natured nicknames for her – 'the Rottweiler' and 'the Crusher'. (I used to call Joe 'the greyhound', as he was always disappearing at top speed!) Sometimes I'd show people a picture of a Rottweiler and tell them it was my mother-in-law. It was all in good fun, though; we got on really well and she was proud of the two of us. She would always refer to us as 'my daughter and my son-in-law' and we both miss her terribly now she is no longer with us. Shirley was like a mother to me, and when she died it was the worst year in Lisa's life.

Another of our holiday 'hot spots' is Milan, the northern Italian city often called the 'fashion capital of the world'.

With a nickname like that, we could hardly miss it off our list …

One of our first visits there came about after I decided to give Lisa a surprise. She thought we were going from Malaga to Barcelona for a short break, and it was only when we got to the airport that she realised we were off to Italy – shades of her fooling me over Mauritius! I handed her 1,000 Euros and told her, 'Don't spend it on coffee.' That brief trip cost a lot more than that, I can tell you. We stayed near the cathedral in the centre of the city and we were close to all those wonderful arcades full of designers like Dolce and Gabbana, Gucci and Versace, plus a load more I've never heard of. Milan is so classy that even the old boys in their nineties look like Robert de Niro in his prime. The day after we arrived we went out and hit the shops. After a while, I'd had enough; I couldn't take any more. I ended up just sitting it out in a restaurant while Lisa carried on by herself. When she returned it was like a scene out of the Julia Roberts film *Pretty Woman*. Lisa walked through the door carrying at least eight designer bags full of clothes. We ended up back at the hotel at 1am with Lisa giving me a fashion show of everything that she had bought. There was no beach nearby for us to get romantic on that time … but we improvised and ended up making love on the balcony of our hotel room at three in the morning!

Then it was back to the shopping. I bought Lisa a lovely white coat for about 5,000 Euros and bought myself a nice Dolce and Gabbana pin-striped jacket and trousers. All in all, I guess I got through about £15,000 during the weekend.

Lisa's sister rang at one stage and suggested that we should go and have a look at the film star George Clooney's place at Lake Como, which is north of Milan. We thought it was a great idea, so I went to get some cash from a hole-in-the-wall ... and it was rejected. What a disaster. Me, a millionaire and unable to get my money out! It was Saturday by this time and that meant we faced the weekend without any cash. Fortunately, I had another card on me that got us through the weekend.

It was only when I got home on the Monday that I received a call from the bank who had declined my card. It was a security check and they were worried about the level of spending on the card in a country where I didn't even live. They must have put an emergency 'stop' on the card until they had checked me out. You can't fault them for their efficiency, but it meant we never got to see Mr Clooney's pad!

Milan also holds a fond place in our memories as Lisa and I were filmed there when we appeared in *Marbella Belles*, the ITV television documentary about the lives of a group of women living in Marbella. If I say so myself, and even though I'm biased, there was no doubt that Lisa was the star of the series. We both played up to the camera a bit, as everybody does, but it was essentially us on screen.

Anyway, the TV crew decided to come with us when they heard that we were going shopping to Italy and they captured it on film, including the incident where Lisa 'forgot' our little son Blue because she was too busy packing. (No, I haven't mentioned him before, have I? Well, you'll hear plenty more about him in the next chapter!) It was during that Milan trip that she went on one of her craziest shopping expeditions. We were in one boutique for an eternity as she tried on outfit after outfit; I thought we'd never get out of there. She was there so long that I turned to Blue – who was just a baby at the time – and told him, 'The next outfit your mother comes out wearing, we'll say that we like it!' I hoped that Lisa would then buy it and we could get out of the place.

She appeared from the changing room and I immediately began waxing lyrical, telling her how marvellous she looked and how much it suited her. She gave me a look and said simply, 'You silly bastard, it's the one I came in wearing!'

While we were in Italy we had a taxi driver to take us into town and he kept looking in his rear-view mirror at us. Eventually he couldn't contain his curiosity any more and asked us who we were – we seemed familiar to him, he said. The film-crew guy who was in the front of the cab couldn't resist a joke and said to him, 'Don't you recognise them? It's Rod Stewart and Penny Lancaster!' The guy seemed to take it on board and for the rest of the journey he was tapping out on the wheel and humming the tune 'Do Ya Think I'm Sexy?' Well, it was an easy mistake to make …

19

Highs and Lows

I honestly feel younger now than I did 40 years ago. Back then, when I was a young guy, I felt about 60. I had the worries of the world on my shoulders and there seemed no light at the end of the tunnel. But that was then, this is now. I feel fitter, and more full of the joys of life, than I ever did.

Obviously, the money has played a part in that. But meeting and marrying Lisa, with the added joy of my stepson Alfie, has played a tremendous part in giving me a new lease of life – and that's putting it mildly. There is one other thing that has transformed me: his name is Blue John Joseph Johnson.

That, as you must have realised by now, is my youngest son, a little bundle of happiness who came into our lives on 21 November 2005. Perhaps he was the result of that romantic trip to Milan we'd made earlier in the year; one thing was for sure, though, we were both over the moon about the news. Lisa had had a miscarriage in late 2001, after which she immediately stopped working at Angels. This time, we had all kinds of tests done to make sure nothing would go wrong during the pregnancy. We even took videos of the scan she had – we've got about 20 of Blue so far, including some taken before he was born. We were so determined that nothing would go wrong, we even agreed to both give up smoking, at the doctor's suggestion – not that we've kept to it, I'm afraid.

Little Blue came into the world under the care of Dr Berral at a private hospital in Marbella (we didn't care how much the hospital bill came to – who would of they had my kind of money?) by Caesarean birth. Alfie was the first to see him. I stayed the night on a sofa in the hospital and Lisa was there for three days in total.

His name was chosen by Josie's daughter Fifi, who was eight at the time. She said, 'If it's a boy, why not call him Blue?' and we agreed. It fitted him perfectly, as he had, and still has, the bluest eyes you have ever seen in your life. Pure magic. It could be that I will be picking him up from school one day while I'm on a Zimmer frame. I don't care: you are only as old as you feel and I feel very, very young.

Soon after Blue was born we considered moving back to England – mainly for family reasons, to be near both our sets of relatives – so we looked at some properties including a converted barn near Epping. The grown-up children were overjoyed at the thought of Dad coming back home. When we came over to finalise the deal, however, it was miserable – non-stop rain – and Lisa and I looked at each other with, 'Are you thinking what I'm thinking?' expressions. Back in the

UK it can be dark at 5pm and all there is to do is stay indoors and watch *Coronation Street*, while back in Spain at 8pm you can be outside sipping a drink at a beach bar. Okay, perhaps we should have a little place in England, but we have such a good circle of friends in Spain – Michelle, John, Jan, Terry, Leeza, Rob, Kathy, Francine, Adam, Margaret, Solly, Ross and Sandy, to name a few – and we all look after each other so well, that we don't need to be based in England.

Anyway, if we had been living in Essex then Lisa might not have become a television star either … She was in her hairdresser's in Puerto Banus one day when her stylist said he had heard about a television programme that was in the pipeline, featuring British women who lived in the area. Would Lisa mind if he passed on her number to someone who knew the programme-makers?

To cut a long story short, the television people got in touch and a man came to see Lisa to do a dry run with her. Off he went and that was that, we didn't hear anything for a while. We gathered on the grapevine that other women had been seen by the makers too and so we didn't think too much of it; we thought they had decided to choose them instead of Lisa. Then the programme people got in touch again and told Lisa, 'You're the one we want.' One of Lisa's reservations was that she might not be the right sort of person for television because she swears – occasionally, not all the time. They told her not to worry – and they were right to take that attitude, as she turned out to be the star of the show.

They filmed from September to December 2006 and we

wouldn't have missed it for the world. It was great fun and – I know this sounds strange, given that they have a film crew in the room with you – it was also all very natural. I even featured in it a few times, and, as I've always been a bit of an exhibitionist in some ways, that was fine with me too. The first two episodes of the series on ITV 1 did give one false impression though; they made out that Lisa was a bad mother and that she forgot all about Blue sometimes. Nothing could be further from reality.

Everyone loved the show and practically no one had a bad word to say to us about it. There were even suggestions that if they did another series it should be called 'The Lisa and Joe Show'. That's probably taking it a bit too far, but it's obvious we managed to come across as larger-than-life on screen.

After the show started broadcasting, we began to be recognised wherever we met. One day we took little Blue to the Tivoli World amusement park, not far from our home in Spain. All of a sudden I heard a voice saying, 'Hello Blue, you're getting big.' So not only had Lisa and I caught the attention of people, even Blue was turning into a star! Another time we were flying by EasyJet from Malaga to Stansted – yes, we don't always fly Club Class around the world – and, like a lot of people, our baggage was over the allowance. So I had to go to the excess baggage section and pay about £14 for being over the limit. As I'm handing the money over, this man in the queue – whom I'd never seen before – chipped in with, 'Don't worry, you can afford it – you're loaded!' To this day, I don't know whether he was being kind or taking the mickey.

A lot of people did wonder how I could afford to live the lifestyle I had on the Costa Del Sol and a lot of speculation began to appear on the Internet about what I did for a living. There were even suggestions that I might be a drug dealer! Throughout my life I've always felt that people could think whatever they wanted to about me, and I wasn't going to be upset or annoyed by their views. It really is a case of 'water off a duck's back' with me. As long as the people I care about hold me in high regard, that's all that counts – the others can take a running jump. But this was different: I had a young family who might in some way suffer if the wrong story started to circulate and I didn't want these false rumours spreading.

So I did a newspaper interview in which I revealed that my Lottery win was the reason I'd got a few bob in the bank and how I'd kept my win a secret from Lisa until I was sure it was me she was interested in, not my money. The secret was finally out and all those people around the pool in Puerto Banus who'd been wondering how I came to live the life I did now knew the answer. Virtually all of them thought it was great. After all, why should it matter to them how I'd come about my money? Would it have been any different if I'd been in insurance, or was a City boy, or a professional gambler? The means by which I'd acquired the good things in life aren't important; it's how you behave once you have them that counts.

By and large, we've got on very well with the people living near us in Spain, but there has been the odd problem. One day, soon after one of the early episodes of *Marbella Belles* was screened, we went down to have a coffee at the poolside restaurant in Alcazaba. I said 'hello' to one of the chaps there, whom I'd been pretty friendly with in the past, and he just ignored me. I said words to the effect of, 'You're very quiet today,' and he replied, 'Yes, sometimes I feel like being quiet.' We were being shunned because of the programme – totally blanked. It was all because of *Marbella Belles* – this guy didn't like it, for some reason. Whether he thought it lowered the tone of the area, I have no idea.

It annoyed me, and it played on my mind a lot, especially as I had done a lot for several people in the area and was always willing to help. Even a five-year-old kid could have seen that the programme wasn't depicting the real Lisa – she was playing up to the camera an awful lot. Who doesn't when they are on 'reality' television? Eventually, I went up to the man's son-in-law and asked him, 'Why are your family so rude, why aren't they talking to us?' He said it was to do with the programme but insisted it had nothing to do with him the way the family was reacting. I told him to do us all a favour and tell his father-in-law and the rest of the family that they didn't even have to acknowledge us in future, we wouldn't mind one little bit. And we haven't spoken to them from that day to this.

Another time, a guy we would often talk to heard that we wanted to sell one of the properties we had bought in Spain. We had hoped it would be a good investment, but it was turning into a bit of a financial thorn in our side. He went to view it with another good friend of ours and said to him, 'Let's nick it off them' – meaning make us a very low offer. The good friend told me about the remark and I went down to the restaurant and told the guy what I thought about him. I didn't hit him or anything like that, but I was really annoyed.

Also, a year after moving to Puerto Banus, I decided I'd start going to a gym. I thought I'd get fit, tone myself up and put on a little bit of muscle. Nothing wrong with that at all. At one stage I found myself working out next to Dolph Lundgren, the Danish film star best known for his role in the *Rocky* films, who also happens to live in Marbella. I told my personal trainer, 'If you need anything, let me know.' Now, I did not mean that financially, more in the general sense of being of assistance, but people were aware that I had a bob or two to my name, even if they didn't know how I'd come by it.

The next thing I knew, he was asking me for money to help him move home. I ended up handing over £10,000 to help the guy. For three weeks he paid me back – then suddenly he just stopped. I went round to see him a few times about it ... then, one day, I saw him driving around in a white Mercedes and I realised what was going on; he was using my money to finance himself and his lifestyle! Lisa rang his wife up and had a pretty frank talk with her. It took us two years, but we got our money back, although now we don't talk to them. You could say I was in a learning curve when it came to money at the time. But my attitude was this: I grew up with nothing and that means I know what it's like to have nothing; I know what it's like to be in trouble. I like to help my fellow man out. I was an ordinary layman; I had not worked my socks off for the money I came into. It came to me as a gift.

Sure, if I could turn the clock back I might do things differently when it came to money. I'd probably put more of it into property and also look at the people I gave or lent money to in a different light. But that's the way life goes.

People ask what it's like living in this lovely part of the world without having the chore of going to work every day – and the answer is, of course, it is marvellous. The first year that we were here it was like one extended holiday – spending time by the pool or on the beach and, to my delight, after a year Lisa said she was happy and wanted to stay.

Throughout this time we had to look after Alfie's education. For the first year he went to an international school in nearby San Pedro, but then he got into an excellent school called Swan's College in Marbella. Despite our charmed lifestyle, that meant that we had to do the everyday things that any parents do: making sure your child gets to school on time and being there to collect him or be home when he returns. You also have to go to all the various school functions – Alfie's crazy about football in general and Chelsea in particular, so we take him to football training. We lead a normal life in that respect, the only difference seems to be that in the UK you would do all that and it's then about 7.30 at night; in Spain you look at the clock and somehow it's 11pm already. Time just whizzes past so quickly here.

Sure, we would go down to the shops and boutiques and buy designer gear some of the time, but in that first year we had lots of visitors too that we had to look after. Some of them were great; some would be idiots, for want of a better word. I don't mean to sound unkind, but we felt we had to take them out at night and organise things for them to do. As a Lottery winner I feel obliged, in a way, to get the bill. I'm not going to name names, that wouldn't be fair. It could be my lot, Lisa's lot, friends, call them what you will, but there were times when you felt that they were taking the piss out of you, to be frank. Perhaps it played on my mind too much, but whenever the bill came, no one chirped up and said, 'How much was that then?' or, 'Shall we split it?' Lisa's brother-in-law was an exception to this: either I'd say, 'It's my turn for the bill' or he would do the honours, so there was never any problem there. It could be that you can't blame people for thinking like that and acting like that. I'd like to think I'd do it a bit differently, though.

That first year or so we did push the boat out quite a bit, probably spending more than when we first got married. It was rings here, jewellery there. We'd get handbags and coats. There is a Cartier in Marbella and we couldn't resist going in there. I bought a lovely Gucci leather jacket down the port and spent £1,000 on another leather jacket that, to be honest, I hardly wear. You haven't got the weather for those sort of clothes, to begin with, and pretty soon they are out of date. We could easily spend £1,000 or £2,000 a week on luxury items, mainly clothes, or eating out, or jewellery. I'm willing to take the blame: if I see something I like I buy it – I don't go shopping around. I can't be bothered to travel 25 miles the next day to buy something there because it's 2p cheaper, that's not for me. If you like it, f**king well get it!

I'll give you an example to illustrate what it was like. We were staying in one night, relaxing with a glass of wine and watching a film, *Shirley Valentine*, about a middle-aged housewife played by Pauline Collins, who falls in love with Cyprus and develops a thing about one of the locals, played by Tom Conti. We loved the look of the place as we sat there looking at the television and decided, 'Okay – let's go to Cyprus!'

I phoned one of our dearest friends, Janice, who lives there, and she sorted out a hotel, the five-star Elysium in Paphos, and a car for two weeks for Lisa, myself and our Colombian friend Alicia, who came to look after Alfie and Blue. Some people sit down in February and plan their holidays for August; we were never like that. We just did it on the spur of the moment.

When you are organising these things, you never think about whether you are going 'over the top', you just get on with arranging them and choosing the deal. It's only afterwards that you look back and think that perhaps you might have gone a bit wild. In one sense we always tried to set ourselves budgets … but we're not really 'budget people'. We might cut down on the price of a tin of beans and then spend £300 on a tin of something else. We love our food and we would eat from the top price of the menu sometimes, but often – and remember, we're both London people – we love our pie, mash and liquor, and there is a place near our Spanish home where I always have their bubble and squeak. In fact, when we'd go to Morrison's in Gibraltar we would shout to each other, 'Look – smoked haddock!' People would look at us and think we'd gone mad or something. They'd have great things like chopped fruit and prepared trifles. I think Lisa buys unnecessary things on these spending sprees – she disagrees with me, of course! – and she can easily fill up two trolleys. She will spend 300 Euros on shopping, and when you go to the cupboard to look in it soon after, there's f**k all there!

Then we reached a stage – and Lisa is better at doing this than me – where, we would have spent quite a lot, so we'd say, 'Let's tighten our belts for a bit.' And we'd watch what we spent – for a while, at least. Inevitably, however, the moment would come when I'd say, 'Oh come on, let's go out tonight' or, 'Let's go away for a bit', and off we'd go again – credit cards at the ready.

There have been some grim times in Spain too, and I guess in any story recalling our life together it would be wrong to miss out some of those, shall we say, 'downbeat' periods. It would be less than honest to do so.

Towards the end of 2003, Lisa and I split up briefly.

There was no one else involved; it's just that things got strained between us. Looking back on it all now, it seems very strange. I suppose I didn't like Lisa going out around Puerto Banus with her girlfriends. It's hard to put it into words why that was, it's just something that I felt uncomfortable with, and that led to tensions between us. We were living in each other's pockets as it was and I guess I made the mistake of wanting her to myself all the time. I didn't like it and she didn't like the fact that I had a thing about this. Perhaps I wanted too much control, perhaps I was unsure of myself. My past started to come back to me and I became both insecure and over-possessive. I was certain I didn't want to lose her, but my behaviour had the opposite effect to the one I wanted.

We had another apartment in the urbanisation and we moved into it while our main apartment was being renovated. We were under the same roof, but because of the strain the marriage was under, we were not sleeping together. When our apartment was ready for us to move back, Lisa went and I stayed where I was. This 'split' lasted about four months in total ... and during that period I seriously wanted to end my life. It got so bad that at one stage I took an overdose of Rohypnol and had to spend a night recovering in a Marbella hospital after having my stomach pumped out. Whether it was a cry for help, or something else, I don't know. I felt so low that it seemed the only thing I could do.

Eventually, we had a meeting and decided that we might as well get lawyers involved and sort it all out. I got in my car afterwards and drove off one way and Lisa got in her car and drove in the opposite direction. Then, thank goodness, Lisa flashed her headlights at me, I stopped, and we started talking again.

I'd moved to a house nearby by this time and I invited her to come and have a look at it. I showed Lisa around the house and she started to cry while she was there. I felt terrible; I genuinely can't articulate how bad I was feeling. Eventually she went home, though not before I suggested we have dinner to discuss everything.

I booked a table at Reginas, one of the best restaurants in the area, and when I took her there the place was covered in flowers. Every type of bouquet you could think of, stunning colours, delicate scents – it blew you away as you walked through the door. Lisa said that she thought it was a beautiful floral display and wondered why they were there. 'They are for you,' I told her. They weren't part of anything the restaurant was involved in, they were flowers that I'd ordered just for her and had arranged to be there for her. Then she got the giggles, which is always a good sign.

I took her home and she just looked at me and said, 'Come here, you silly bastard!' and with that we kissed. I ended up staying the night and let's just say we got very affectionate and made up for all that lost time.

Thank God we got back together. Life is worth living again – and with a capital 'L' this time, too.

20

A Whole Lotto Love

So, what is life like for a man who's won millions, spent a lot of it on having a good time and lives in one of the most glamorous spots on the globe? Pretty damn good, thank you.

I don't want to sound self-satisfied, but the life I lead is marvellous and there's no denying it – it would be hypocritical to do so. I can't stand those people who moan, 'Oh that big win ruined my life' and all that nonsense. Sure, it brought a few problems with it, but I'd had problems before, so that was nothing new. It also brought me great happiness and the start of a period of my life that I still find borders on the unbelievable. At a time when most men are winding down and wondering whether they've got enough money to last them the rest of their days, I suddenly struck gold in every sense of the world. Why, even my looks have changed.

I don't mind admitting it, I'm a bit of a vain bastard at times. I always liked nice clothes and looking good, even in the days when I couldn't really afford it. So, once the money came along, it was only right that I spent some of it on sprucing myself up. I'd got the clothes and the jewellery, but there was one thing that it took me a while to get around to – my face.

Shortly before we moved to Spain, Lisa's sister Josie suggested I had some work done on my looks. My son Zak had had some done and he recommended it, so I went to a plastic surgeon in Chelsea. The idea was to take some fat off from under my chin and remove old skin, to 'scrape' it off – but it all went horribly wrong. I had full-face laser treatment that eventually healed but left a bad scar, so I needed another operation. It looked as though somebody had thrown boiling fat in my face! In all I spent £10,000, and it wasn't worth it at all. I wasn't happy needing to have a second operation to try and rectify it, and this time I was awake – which, as I'm sure you can imagine, made it even worse. That was that, I thought, and I decided not to go near a plastic surgeon again, thank you very much.

As always though, things change. After we'd moved to Spain there was that brief interlude when Lisa and I split. She had some breast implants done during this time and the doctor in Marbella did a smashing job, take my word for it! For about £4,000 she had gone from a 34B to a 34C. She also had some botox done and he gave her collagen too. He'd done a terrific job, and it totally restored my faith in what these guys can do – what a contrast from the nightmare I'd been through.

So I decided to give it another go and booked into the same

clinic as Lisa had to use the same excellent French surgeon. He sorted out my chin with a facelift, as well as tidying up my upper and lower eyelids. Oh yes, he also took off a bit of fat from around my nose that Lisa thought looked a bit 'bulbous', as she put it. And then, hey presto, after two days in there I looked a new man. I still feel a little embarrassed talking about it, I don't know why, but overall I'm very pleased with the final result.

To complete the make-over I've also had what you might term 'Di-lights' in my hair on occasions to give me that suntanned look. I did tell you I was vain, though, didn't I?

Yes, a lot of my recent happiness has been generated by money. All those famous-name stores I had only read about – Harrods, Cartier, Rolex – became like Tesco to me: just another shop to pop into and spend some money. The cars I had dreamt of for years were suddenly there outside my door waiting for me to hop into and drive away. And if I got fed up with them – I even had an Aston Martin DB7 for six months that I used to drive around Puerto Banus harbour posing in – then I'd get rid of it and move on to something else. Countries I'd only seen on the television became second homes, and I would take their stunning beauty in my stride – but I didn't take it for granted.

So, how do we spend our time? Sometimes we can be found in Puerto Banus, either shopping or with the children – just like any couple really. We also enjoy dining out at places such as the Villa Tiberius, the Red Pepper and Magna Marbella. We're not massive eaters of Spanish food, but we do like a nice steak or some fish and we love Lobster Thermidor washed down with a good red Rioja or perhaps a bottle of our favourite Cristal champagne. There again, we might wander down to the beach at any time of day, or perhaps go to nearby Benahavís, where we know a place that does superb roast suckling pig.

The wealth I kept secret for so long, and hid from Lisa for what seemed like an eternity, is now public knowledge. My friends and neighbours know all about it and millions of television viewers and newspaper readers are also in on what was once known to just a select handful. On *Marbella Belles* the narrator, Dennis Waterman, commented, 'Joe hasn't got a few quid – he is loaded!' And at the National TV Awards, Harry Hill highlighted in one section from his show the moment when Lisa seemed to forget Blue and couldn't resist quipping that perhaps we'd named our youngest after The Bluewater Shopping Centre!

Sure, we like our shopping. Yes, I have bought Lisa a Cartier *and* a Rolex gold watch at £10,000 each *and* a diamond bracelet from Cartier in Malaga for around the same price – but why shouldn't I? I bought myself a gold Cartier necklace too, just to balance things out, and sometimes we seem to be wearing more Cartier than the company themselves have in their Bond Street storeroom safe.

But, I must admit, there are some aspects of my new life in the sun that I haven't adapted to too well. Shortly after we moved to Spain, Lisa turned to me and said, 'Get a hobby.' I've never been a big hobby type of guy, but she reckoned I needed something to keep me busy and, as this part of the Costa Del Sol is famous for its golf courses, it made sense for me to take up the game. There is a well-known golf school run by a man called John Moncur near me and I had three lessons with him. I wasn't the greatest in the world and Tiger Woods didn't have to start worrying, but nevertheless, I reckoned it was time to buy all the gear.

There are several large golfing stores nearby catering for all the golfing fanatics in the area, so I had no trouble finding what I needed. I spent about £2,000 on the goods altogether – I bought the clubs, the trolley, the clothes – basically everything the novice golfer needed. I was as pleased as punch, but I couldn't be bothered to load it all in the car, so I had them delivered.

Sure enough, soon afterwards, the items arrived and I was as happy as a sandboy unpacking them … until I discovered one important item was missing: I'd only got one glove, instead of a pair. Lisa said, 'What a f**king liberty! Go back and get the other one.' Off I went in a cloud of dust back to the store and stormed in. I wasn't in the mood to take prisoners – just because I was a newcomer to this golf business didn't mean they could take advantage of me. It was either that, or inefficiency on their part, and I wasn't going to stand for that either.

'That golf gear you sent me,' I began, 'there is a glove missing!' For a while there was silence and then the salesman quietly told me not to be too upset, you only wear one glove when you play golf. Oh dear, talk about making a fool of myself. They managed to keep a straight face as they told me, but I hate to think what they said after I left the shop. When I told Lisa she just looked at me and said, 'You f**king idiot!' After that inauspicious start it's hardly surprising that I never really took to the sport – the golf clubs ended up slung in the garage gathering dust.

Fishing is another big pastime in Spain. It is loved by tourists and locals alike. Every spot of beach or rocks seems to have a Spaniard on it trying to catch some fresh fish. So I thought I'd have a go at that too. I bought a state-of-the-art set of eight rods … and I'm sure you can guess where they ended up. That's right, alongside the golf clubs in the garage! I do take them out on occasions, but only to give them a dust down; I never seem to get round to using them.

Despite my luxurious surroundings, there is still a bit of the gypsy in me. Once, when I was 'Poor Joe' and Lisa didn't know of my wealth, we went on a wonderful holiday to a caravan park in Devon with Nick and his family. It was fantastic, even though it was winter and I was having to pretend to be poor. We kept warm with an electric fire and sleeping bags, but we didn't mind. There was an indoor swimming pool at the site and a social club and a cabaret every evening; it was such good fun. If we wanted to eat we'd have fish and chips or a Chinese, Cornish pasties or a traditional West Country tea. I even managed to come up trumps with my gambling again. It wasn't £10 million this time, but £120 at the clubhouse bingo isn't bad. I was really excited when all my numbers came up and I shouted 'House!' at the top of my voice. I shared my winnings with Nick's son Jamie, as we'd gone halves on the game. It is silly, I know, for a grown man who had won a fortune to get enthusiastic about a caravan site game of bingo, but that's the way I am.

The next time we went to the same site it was a bit different. Lisa and I were married and my secret was out – I was now officially 'Rich Joe'. So instead of a rusty old caravan, we went in the six-berth Winnebago I'd bought for about £50,000. I didn't like it too much when I first got it. But by the time I'd added a few extras – cycle racks on the back, a TV, a cocktail bar and a shower – and got it kitted out in superb fashion, I thought it was great.

Now we just had to find somewhere to use the damn thing. We decided to ask Lisa's brother John, his wife Maria and his two children – plus the dog, Marcus – to come to Devon with us. It was the end of the summer and we had a fantastic time.

Lisa knowing about my win wasn't the only difference between the trips. When we'd gone the first time, we parked the caravan up, unhooked the car, and then could head off to wherever we wanted. With the Winnebago, it's a lot more complicated: you have to plug it into the electricity and the water connections, so you can't just pop off in it at the drop of a hat. But, we didn't think of any of this beforehand, so, unless we went through the long and tiring procedure of detaching the Winnebago, we were without transport!

One day we decided to go into nearby Ilfracombe and John suggested we simply jump on the local bus. So that's what we did. All the people on the bus were locals, not a tourist in sight; it was a great laugh – there we were worth millions, riding along on a bus on our holiday alongside pensioners on the way to pick up their money! We spent the day in Ilfracombe wandering around and seeing the sights and had a great time. Mind you, when it came to getting back to the campsite we decided it would be quicker to jump in two taxis and pay £10 rather than wait for the country bus.

Some things don't change, though. I guess we could have taken a *Good Food Guide* with us and gone to the finest restaurants in the West Country if we'd wanted to; I didn't have to keep anything secret from Lisa now. But we ended up doing exactly what we'd done last time, when I was just 'Poor Joe' taking a break in the caravan: fish-and-chip dinners and evenings down the social club playing bingo. The only difference this time was that I didn't win. Life just isn't fair, is it?

We decided that the next time we went away in the Winnebago it would be on our own – by that I mean Lisa, Alfie and myself. In the dead of winter we chose to go to Brighton. Perhaps not one of the better decisions I've made in my life. The weather was horrible and we couldn't get the bloody heater to work, which meant the inside of the vehicle was freezing. Lisa decided to have a shower, not just to clean up, but to warm up too. First of all the water was lovely and warm and she was as happy as could be in there. Then, all of a sudden, I head her screaming that the water had suddenly stopped being hot and had turned icy cold. She stormed out of the shower and announced, 'That's my last camping holiday – never again!' She had made her mind up.

I couldn't fix the heater or get the hot water working. It would probably have been simple enough to do, but I just didn't know how. In desperation I dug out the handbook and frantically started flicking through the pages. It seemed to be in gibberish and it took me a second or two to realise why – it wasn't in English. It seemed to all be in French, presumably because at some stage the vehicle had been intended for the French market. But that didn't do me much good, and I wasn't in the position to do a crash course in French. I know I should have looked at it when I bought the vehicle, but there didn't seem to be any need then.

We had a big row about it and that was that – we packed up and came straight back home. When Alfie woke up he was back at Blackhall, not down at Brighton; he must have wondered what was going on. I parked the vehicle round the back at Blackhall and no amount of persuading would convince Lisa to try another holiday in it. She was totally adamant that it was a 'no go'.

After a couple of months I got rid of it, at a terrific loss. I drove down to Bournemouth and sold it to a motor-home place there. Mind you, before we did, we lent it to my son-in-law's parents and they had a fantastic time touring Scotland in it. No doubt they did the sensible thing and figured out how it all worked before setting off …

I still haven't ruled out the idea of buying another one at some stage in the future. It's always been one of my dreams to just throw together a few clothes and drive off on a whim; I guess it's the lure of the open road. The good thing is that now we're living in a warm climate like Spain it might be a lot more appealing to Lisa. I know she said hell would freeze over before she went camping again, but 'never say never' as they say. If I do get one, ne thing is for sure, though: I'll make sure the handbook n English ...

At the moment I'm busy organising a birthday party for Lisa and that will probably set me back the usual £10,000 or so for the night. Our plan is to hire a villa so that there is plenty of room for everyone to eat, drink, dance the night away and then catch a few hours' sleep before starting all over again. We've had a look at a few – including one that *X-Factor* judge Simon Cowell has used in the past – but sorry, they didn't come up to scratch.

If all this came to an end somehow, if the money and the cars and the homes vanished overnight, we would still have each other. We could live in a one-bedroom flat and still be happy. You don't need big houses to be content; there is more to life than that. Anyway, both Lisa and I have had to earn a living for most of our lives, so it wouldn't be anything new to us. Of course, it's easy for me to say things like that, but I genuinely believe them too.

When I first won my millions I thought I could handle it in every sense of the word, but that was far from the truth – I made a lot of mistakes believing I could deal with the money when I wasn't really capable of doing so. It was 'new' money to me. I wasn't worried about bills or budgets or anything like that; I just went at it like a bull in a china shop. I knew that I had enough to last me a lifetime and that was all I cared about, but I'd do a lot of things differently now, given the knowledge of life and people I've accumulated since my win.

I guess you might want to ask how much I have got left in the kitty … my answer would be that it's no one's business but mine and Lisa's! We're never going to starve, though. I haven't got as much as that day in May 1998 when the big one came in and those Lucky Dip numbers 8, 20, 24, 35, 43, 47 changed my life forever. I have wasted quite a chunk of that cash bonanza, true, but I also gave a sizeable part of it to my children and I don't regret that for an instant.

Lisa and I have got to pull our belts in now and then, but we still have enough to last us both comfortably for the rest of our days while we live in a beautiful home in idyllic surroundings. That can't be bad, can it?

I sit here in Spain as the sun blazes in through the window and look around at the pleasure that surrounds me. As well as Lisa there are our boys Alfie and Blue, Lin-Lin our Filipino nanny and our beautiful five-year-old pedigree Shar Pei bitch called Lou Lou. I'm a content man indeed. Lisa loves Spain too, but having said all that, if she wanted to move back to England I would not bat an eyelid.

But I never lose sight of where I came from or the hard times I had in my life. Nor do I forget those who helped me when I was down, when I literally needed favours simply to keep body and soul together. We have spent money on the good things in life – cars, jewellery, holidays – but we don't flaunt our fortune in the faces of others who are less well-off. We don't feel impressed or overawed by the money of other people; instead, we save our deepest respect for the people who haven't got what we have – the mothers and fathers who get up early to go to work as cleaners or in factories to help look after their families.

As you may have gathered by now, Lisa and I still have our ups and downs. No married couple on earth can say otherwise, can they? If such a pairing does exist, I've never come across them. Only recently we had a storming row for 30 minutes before setting off to Rome for one of our much-loved breaks. I ended up saying to Lisa, 'All right then, I won't go!' And, surprise, surprise, she took me at my word. Without wasting a second she was on the phone to the travel agent and substituted Alfie's name for mine. I took them to the airport and by the time we got there I was telling her, 'I wish I could change my mind …' But it was too late, I couldn't alter the ticket so near to take-off time and there were no other ones available. Of course, I missed her the instant she was out of sight – and it was mutual. No sooner was she in her hotel in Rome than she was on the telephone to me saying how much she missed me.

Sometimes I look upon Lisa as a stallion in a field waiting to be tamed. Before anyone says anything clever, yes, I am aware that a stallion is a male horse, but she has that magnificent air about her that goes with such a beast. Every time you try and take control, she just throws you off; there seems no way at first that she can be controlled. I know I will never take that spirit out of her. I don't want to and it's mission impossible anyway. I am not out to tame her – I couldn't – but I will master her in some way. At least, I hope so.

That's the story so far, but to answer one final, obvious question: yes, I still do the Lottery most weeks. Years ago I felt confident that I'd win it one day, and I did. The funny thing is, I still have the same feeling. I really believe I will strike gold again and, don't you worry, when I do I'll know exactly what to do with my second £10 million. But, rest assured, if I do get lucky, I'll tell you all about it.

The one thing I know for sure, with a greater certainty than I can ever put in words, is this: the biggest win I've ever had in the lottery of life was finding the love of my life … Lisa.